ADVAN

"Aging well involves paying attention to our lifestyle and all the factors that can potentially impact it. Our financial well-being is definitely one of those factors. Jason Smith's *The Bucket Plan* provides the right questions to ask and considerations needed to design a structured and comprehensive plan that will allow you to pursue a life of being all you can be."

—Roger Landry, MD, MPH, award-winning author of *Live Long, Die Short: A Guide to Authentic Health and Successful Aging*

"Jason Smith's *The Bucket Plan* does a great job of distilling a wealth of sophisticated retirement planning wisdom into a simple story that anyone can understand. Read this, and let Jason open your eyes to the advantages of 'bucketing' your money to achieve the most successful financial plan to support the future you want, now, soon, and in the distant future."

—Dan Sullivan, founder, The Strategic Coach, Inc.

"*The Bucket Plan* is an easy-to-read, thought-provoking book that takes the reader on a journey that many of us wish we could travel. Jason Smith uses his creative genius to tell the story of a process that simplifies the often complex world of personal finance. In doing so, he demonstrates the peace of mind and understanding of our financial concerns that Americans approaching or in retirement long to achieve."

—John Gilliam, PhD, MBA, CFP®, CLU®, department of personal financial planning, Texas Tech University

"Jason Smith's book is one of the best in the business. The Bucket Plan® planning process is absolutely the best way to serve your clients and motivate them to implement. Jason's insights and processes are far and away above all others."

—Kerry Johnson, PhD, MBA, best-selling author, speaker, and coach

THE BUCKET PLAN

Protecting and Growing Your Assets for a Worry-Free Retirement

Based on a True Story

With Foreword by "America's IRA Expert" Ed Slott

JASON L SMITH

Published by Greenleaf Book Group Press
Austin, Texas
www.gbgpress.com

Distributed by Greenleaf Book Group

For ordering information or special discounts for bulk purchases, please contact Greenleaf Book Group at PO Box 91869, Austin, TX 78709, 512.891.6100.

Design and composition by Greenleaf Book Group and Sheila Parr
Cover design by Greenleaf Book Group and Sheila Parr
Cover image ©Nicholas 852 / Shutterstock

Printed in the United States of America on acid-free paper

The information contained in this book is intended to provide helpful and informative material on the subjects addressed. It is not intended to serve as a replacement for professional advice. Any use of the information in this book is at the reader's discretion. Although the author and publisher have made every effort to ensure the information in this book was correct at press time, the author and publisher do not assume and hereby disclaim any liability to any party for any loss, damage, or disruption caused by errors or omissions, whether such errors or omissions result from negligence, accident, or any other cause.

Client names, circumstances, and other personal information included in this book have been changed to protect privacy.

To all the advisors in The Mastermind Group who contributed to the development of The Bucket Plan® planning process: Thank you for your hard work and dedication. You are truly making a difference in the lives of countless American families across this great country of ours.

Most people don't plan to fail; they fail to plan.
—John J. Beckley

CONTENTS

PREFACE

Upon graduation from St. Mary's College in CA on a Saturday in 1994, I joined the financial services profession and started my financial planning practice the following Monday. Helping people accomplish their financial goals is all I have ever done. During my career, I had the opportunity to meet Jason L Smith, the creator of The Bucket Plan®—a philosophy that helps strategically segment and allocate a client's assets to eliminate major investment and retirement risks while creating more efficiency in their financial and estate plan. When Jason first walked me through the process, I quickly realized it could change people's lives. Over my career, I have experienced three major stock market downturns to include the dot com bubble of 2001, the great recession of 2008 and 2009, and the most recent market downturn during COVID-19. Having guided all of my clients through these market cycles, I can really see the power of *The Bucket Plan*.

The Bucket Plan Provides Peace of Mind

In my practice, I work with a diverse group of clients who come from different backgrounds and life stages. *The Bucket Plan* offers strategic solutions to their financial questions. Whether it's high net worth families looking for ways to optimize their wealth, families approaching retirement, or seniors wanting a sense of security through their retirement and an efficient legacy plan, *The Bucket Plan* helps provide them with answers.

In one case, I met with a widowed woman. She had accumulated substantial assets and had plenty of retirement income, but was concerned about how her money would transition to her only daughter when she passed away. Her estate was unorganized with accounts at many different financial institutions, beneficiary designations missing, and no one coordinating everything for her. Through The Bucket Plan planning process, I was able to show her how to structure her accounts to continue to provide reliable income throughout her retirement, as well as ensure all the assets would pass on to her daughter in the most tax efficient manner. That simple process changed her life, and after years of worry, she finally had real clarity and sense of security about the legacy she would leave behind. After completing the process, she referred her daughter and son-in-law to meet with me to ensure we had a multi-generational plan in place for the family, and *The Bucket Plan* was our common language between the two generations. Regardless of your net worth, age or objectives, I am confident you will find The Bucket Plan philosophy detailed within these pages to be a solid foundation for your immediate, short- and long-term financial goals.

I hope you enjoy the book!

—Christopher T. McClure, CRPC®, CBEC®
Lincoln Financial Advisors

FOREWORD

You are reading this book because you want a secure retirement, free from worry, stress, and confusion. *The Bucket Plan* is a must-read book for anyone serious about creating a practical and sensible financial plan for his or her retirement years.

Unlike most books on retirement planning, you'll read this all the way through in a few hours, and you won't want to put it down. Each chapter builds on the previous chapters. As you continue reading, you will start to see a plan forming. That's because Jason L Smith, the author, has created a process so that nothing falls through the cracks. The best part of learning about The Bucket Plan® is that there are very few moving parts. That means less confusion and more understanding. You'll learn more here than you would from most other retirement books, probably because you'll never get to the end of them. They're too long and offer too many options, leaving you wondering if there is any solution at all that you can actually use.

The Bucket Plan is that solution. It reads so easily because it's a story about a couple, Jerry and Irene, to whom you will immediately relate. You'll like them! They are just like you and your friends. They have worked, built savings, and now want to plan for a successful retirement.

As you read, you'll find yourself going through the same thinking process and understanding the reasons for the three-bucket strategy. You'll see that Jerry and Irene's concerns are like yours, and you'll start seeing your own solutions appear.

Your biggest questions about retirement will be answered,

such as, "Will I have enough money? How much income will I need now, soon, and later?" Those are the three buckets, and you'll also look at how each of those buckets should be invested, according to your own comfort level. You won't have to take chances or rely on luck, as unfortunately many people do.

Jason L Smith immediately connects with you and begins by steering you clear of the biggest mistakes people make in planning their retirement. As you keep reading, you'll gain more understanding and confidence about your own retirement plan. The Bucket Plan keeps you on track and eliminates bad choices. To me, that is probably the single biggest benefit of the planning process. Even Jerry and Irene recognized some big mistakes that Jerry's brother Ted made. Avoiding financial mistakes is a big part of building wealth and making it last.

This book is both encouraging and motivating, so much so that you'll want to get to the end of the Jerry and Irene story so that you can implement this immediately with your financial advisor. You won't want to put it off for another minute.

Please set aside a few uninterrupted hours to read this book. After all, you've spent maybe twenty, thirty, or even forty years or more building your savings, so why not spend just a little more time to create a plan to grow, preserve, and protect what you have worked so hard to build? I know when you finish reading, you'll be thinking, "I can do this!" Yes, you can, and that is the beauty of The Bucket Plan. You'll see what I mean.

Let me get out of the way so you can get started. I'm sure you'll enjoy this. I did!

Ed Slott, CPA, Retirement Expert, Founder of
www.irahelp.com

INTRODUCTION

I help people with their investment, insurance, tax, and/or legacy planning and have done so since 1995. Working folks, retirees and pre-retirees, business owners, middle-class millionaires, and ultra-affluent families have all passed through my office doors looking for professional help with their financial planning. All my clients are important to me, but working with one couple—Jerry and Irene[1]—stands out as one of the most meaningful interactions of my career.

Jerry was a very well respected commercial construction manager in our community. When we met, he had recently scaled back his work and was doing some part-time consulting with the goal of retiring in the next two years. Jerry was very excited about his upcoming retirement and wanted to make sure everything was in order so that he and his wife Irene, a semi-retired teacher, wouldn't have to bother with any financial hassles in their later years. When he called the office to make an appointment for our initial consultation, he said to me, "Jason, you and I can just take care of this ourselves. I've always been the one to handle our finances. I'm not sure Irene would even be interested."

While I respected Jerry's desire to spare his wife the details of hammering out a financial plan, I insisted that she be involved from the start. I explained that, if anything were to

---

1 Their real names and other personal information have been altered to protect their privacy.

happen to one of them, the survivor would need to understand the reality of what was going on with their finances. I told him that I take my clients through a comprehensive learning process as we prepare their plans, and I wanted both to receive all the benefits of that education. Once I explained it that way, Jerry agreed with my rationale, and Irene participated in every meeting. To Jerry's delight, Irene turned out to be keenly interested in learning more about their financial situation. She thoroughly enjoyed our meetings and had a great time offering her input and asking questions.

As part of the educational process and the creation of Jerry and Irene's comprehensive financial plan, I used a process called The Bucket Plan® to fact find, analyze, and advise them on their entire financial situation: investments, insurance, taxes, Social Security, and estate planning for when one or both pass away. The financial planning process is based on a three-bucket philosophy of strategically positioning assets to plan for and mitigate the risks and dangers that can occur in retirement. This philosophy is drastically different and much more effective than the old method of planning for retirement. The old method was to keep a little pile of money in the bank and a bigger pile of money in investments—such as IRAs, 401(k)s, stocks, and bonds—and then hope like heck it would be enough to draw on for the rest of your life. Sometimes you'd get lucky, and it would work out in your favor; sometimes it wouldn't. But when you strategically allocate your money using our three-bucket philosophy, you create a plan that mitigates risk *and* offers an opportunity for growth into the future, which allows you to feel more secure about your retirement.

Back to Jerry and Irene. To kick off their planning process, we started by engaging in a conversation about their top priorities, goals, and concerns in retirement. We needed to understand them and their family history to customize their plan based on *their* priorities, not ours. Next, we gathered information about their assets and income sources. We then used an assessment tool to determine if there would be a gap between the amount of money they'd need for day-to-day living during retirement versus the income they'd be receiving each month from Social Security and pensions. We also conducted an analysis to determine their tolerance for market volatility and risk. Once we'd collected all this data and information, we used it to strategically allocate their assets in accordance with The Bucket Plan philosophy, giving them confidence and peace of mind with their finances while simultaneously helping them achieve their goals and expectations for growth going forward.

Among other things, we put in place a life insurance policy that would pay off their mortgage and give some additional liquidity and income replacement to the surviving spouse when the first one passed away. We calculated their future tax liability and made sure we had mechanisms in place to cover all the bases, so there would be no unpleasant surprises from the IRS down the road. We ensured that all their assets were correctly titled and their beneficiaries were properly designated so they wouldn't accidently end up in probate court. And we gathered their important financial information logically in one document so it would be accessible at a moment's notice whenever Jerry and Irene needed it.

Unfortunately, Irene would need it sooner than anyone realized. Within a year of putting together their Bucket Plan, Jerry was killed in a tragic car accident. Irene was suddenly a widow. She was devastated, as was everyone in the community who knew Jerry, including me.

A few days after Jerry's funeral, Irene and I met in my office. She was still in complete shock about the heartbreaking turn her life had taken. I settled her into a chair in my office, took out a marker and her Bucket Plan documents, and began laying everything out for her on the big whiteboard on the wall. I drew three buckets—a Now bucket, a Soon bucket, and a Later bucket. I showed her how the life insurance policy we'd put in place for Jerry would pay off her mortgage completely. I explained that the money allocated for the Now bucket would provide sufficient funds for emergencies or unexpected expenses that might crop up in the near future. I showed her how the Soon bucket we'd set up would supply the next ten years' worth of income. Then I sketched out how the Later bucket we'd established would give her growth and an income for the rest of her life beyond the next ten years, plus ample amounts of other investments to outpace inflation. In short, I showed her that the plan we had created would provide solutions to fill all the financial gaps created by Jerry's sudden and untimely death.

I finished my overview and turned to face Irene. She sat in silence, looking down at the conference table for what seemed like an eternity. At last, she looked up at me with tears rolling down her face, and she said with a decisive nod, "Jason, I'm going to be okay, aren't I?"

"Yes, Irene," I replied. "You are going to be okay, and I will be right here to help you every step of the way."

With that, she stood up, walked over, and gave me the biggest hug I've ever had in my life. Irene's a small lady, but that hug had tremendous power behind it. I must admit that I teared up too. What an incredible feeling to know that I helped a person in need gain some measure of peace during her darkest hour. And what an incredible feeling for Irene to realize that she had the knowledge and the financial plan to live out the rest of her life comfortably. Even now, after all these years, whenever Irene calls the office for advice or comes in for her annual review, I'm reminded of the impact The Bucket Plan can have on people's lives. Folks like Jerry and Irene are the reason I can't wait to get up in the morning and get to work.

My team and I have many more stories like this, and so do the comprehensive financial planners who are part of our Mastermind Group all around the country. But unfortunately, there are countless other stories of pre-retirees and retirees who did not have access to this kind of holistic financial planning and suffered the consequences of paying too much in taxes, being unprepared when the unexpected struck—or, worst of all, running out of money entirely.

The Bucket Plan Mitigates Risk

As you're reading this book, are you confident that the market will only go up from where it is now? In these volatile times, all Americans must have a solid plan for dealing with risk now and in the future. If history has taught us anything, it's that market peaks are at the top of very steep cliffs. Nobody knows for sure what the market will do tomorrow, let alone five years from now. Even though it's fair to predict that the market will keep cycling up over the long term, you need to be prepared for some days, weeks, months, or even years in the abyss. If you're not prepared for these inevitable market corrections, you run the risk of making disastrous mistakes in managing your assets. People who see their assets shrink overnight tend to hit the panic button and move their money to cash at the worst possible time. That is, they sell their investments at a low point and turn a temporary downturn into a catastrophic (and potentially permanent) loss. This problem is most acute for retirees who can't wait out a market correction because they either need steady income or need money to resolve an unexpected event.

When you must pull money out of your investments for income in a market downturn, you're essentially cashing in a larger piece of your portfolio to get the amount of money you need. Ultimately, this leads to one of the biggest dangers people face today: running out of money in retirement.

The Bucket Plan helps you mitigate that risk.

The Bucket Plan is a three-bucket approach to structuring your assets to provide reliable income when you need it and to grow your money over long-term time horizons to battle inflation throughout retirement.

DEBUNKING THE 4 PERCENT RULE

For many years, my team and I have used The Bucket Plan planning process to provide peace of mind to thousands of couples and individuals who are retired or nearing retirement, and they are reaping the benefits of greater financial security because of it. Our clients worry less about what the stock market is doing today and are more confident their assets will provide for them in the future. They can sleep soundly at night because they know they have something their parents and grandparents never had: a plan that addresses the risks and gaps in their retirement finances.

The Bucket Plan is the forward-thinking way of achieving financial security in retirement. It takes all the guesswork and reliance on "luck" out of retirement planning. For example, consider the old rule of thumb that says if you draw no more than 4 percent from your assets during retirement, you'll never run out of money. Many traditional financial advisors still abide by that rule and recommend this strategy to their clients. But a 2013 study by researchers at Texas Tech, the American College, and Morningstar[2] showed that, with current market conditions, even a 3 percent withdrawal rate has a more than 20 percent failure rate. The researchers also found that, for conservative investors with less than 50 percent of their assets in stocks, *the chance of running out of money after 30 years is more than 50 percent!*

Think about those odds for a moment. Imagine you're in line at the airport waiting to board a flight to Key West for some fun in the sun. Suddenly, the pilot steps out and announces, "Welcome, ladies and gentlemen. I am obligated to inform you that this flight has less than a 50 percent chance of making it to Key West safely today." Would you board that plane? Probably not; you'd look for a more dependable flight. Why take chances when you don't have to? Yet that's exactly what many folks are doing when it comes to their retirement "planning."

---

2 Finke, Michael S., Pfau, Wade D., and Blanchett, David M., "The 4% Rule Is Not Safe in a Low-Yield World" (January 15, 2013). Accessed at https://ssrn.com/abstract=2201323 on December 30, 2015.

Running out of money in retirement is no joke, especially when you reach your later years. It is not a pretty scenario. Unfortunately, many of today's retirees are skating on that kind of thin ice because they and their advisors are still operating under the old philosophy of throwing all their assets into one big bucket, withdrawing a set percentage each month, and then crossing their fingers while ignoring the possibility of market downturns. I wouldn't exactly call that a plan. We run into retirees all the time who've been drawing as much as 5, 6, 7, and even 8 percent per year from their investments, and their advisors have never said a word to them about the fact that they will probably run out of money someday. These clients are shocked and nearly fall out of their chairs when we create a customized Bucket Plan for them and show them how much of a risk they've been facing when it comes to running out of money before the end of their lives. It's scary, and it's sad.

As holistic financial planners—that is, professionals who build customized plans that address all aspects of our clients' financial lives (tax, legacy, Social Security, insurance, and investments) as opposed to the traditional broker/advisor who just sells products and portfolios—it's our job to educate you about comprehensive and sound asset-positioning strategies that mitigate investor risk, so you'll be less likely to make bad decisions in volatile times and more likely to grow your money to last into the future. That's what The Bucket Plan planning process does, and that's what this book is all about.

In the pages that follow, I outline our three-bucket approach to positioning your assets effectively. This approach accounts for the very real possibility that you may not always have total control over withdrawal timing and no control over most investing risks. Our attitude is this: If these dynamics cannot be controlled, then they need to be contained by doing a comprehensive financial plan in advance. The Bucket Plan does just that.

In this book, we'll walk alongside an actual couple nearing retirement—Jerry and Irene—as we navigate the process of creating their customized Bucket Plan. It's important to keep in mind that, although we're using a married Baby-Boomer couple as our example here, The Bucket Plan can be applied to anyone. Married, single, divorced, or in a common-law relationship; Generation X or Baby Boomer; affluent or middle class . . . *everyone* can benefit from undertaking the process described in this book, and it's never too early or too late to start. This is what you'll learn about in this book:

- The three biggest dangers you face when planning for your financial future and how The Bucket Plan helps protect you from them.
- The "money cycle" and how it influences your financial decision making.
- How the comprehensive approach taken by holistic financial planners is very different and more effective than that of traditional brokers or advisors.
- A simple questionnaire that helps you and your financial planner find, assess, catalog, and properly position all your liquid investable assets, leading to the creation of your own "personal balance sheet" that makes it easy for your loved ones to settle your affairs when the time comes, helps your survivors avoid probate court, and ensures you don't accidently disinherit your grandkids.

- A clear-cut formula for calculating whether you will have an income deficit in retirement and, if so, how much money you'll need to draw from liquid investable assets to replace your earned employment income.
- A surefire way to avoid taking on too much investment risk on money you may need in the near future.
- The "tax time bomb" that is poised to blow up on your surviving family members and how The Bucket Plan planning process helps you defuse it.
- And much, much more.

The Bucket Plan planning process allows you to enjoy your retirement by letting you focus on the good life: spending time with family and friends; doing the things you love; and worrying less about money, stock market volatility, and the economy. As you'll learn from Jerry and Irene's example, it's a plan that gives you peace of mind.

Let's explore The Bucket Plan planning process and discover how to put it to work for you.

Chapter 1

THE BIGGEST DANGERS YOU FACE IN RETIREMENT

Market Risk, Interest Rate Risk, and Sequence of Returns Risk

Before we dive into a full explanation of the financial dangers facing retirees today and The Bucket Plan® as the solution, let's lay a proper foundation by looking at something everyone goes through during his or her lifetime: the *money cycle.* Knowledge of the money cycle is critical to your understanding of The Bucket Plan and how it can set you up for a secure future.

The money cycle includes three distinct phases we all go through in life: accumulation, preservation, and distribution.

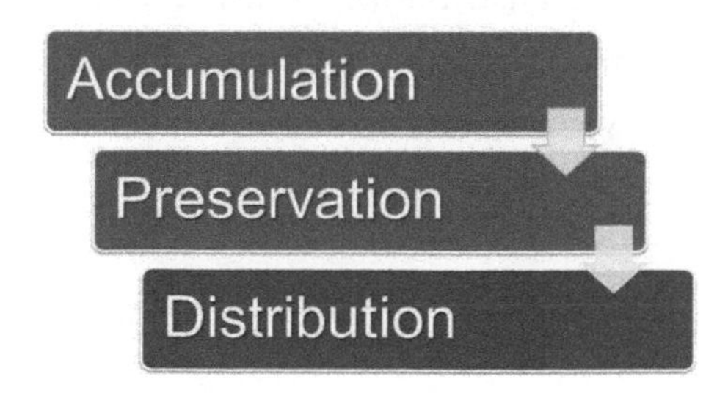

Accumulation usually starts when you're a kid. You've got a piggy bank or a junior checking account where you put your tooth fairy money, birthday cash, babysitting income, money from mowing the lawn, and so on. This accumulation phase continues into adulthood and throughout your working years as you build your life savings. Perhaps you open a retirement savings plan, and maybe your employer even puts money in there for you by matching your contributions. Since you have a long time horizon ahead before you retire, you can afford to take more risks with your money during this stage of your life.

As you get closer to retirement (say, ten years out or less), you move into the *preservation* phase. At this point, you're financially stable and looking forward to winding down your career, effectively ending the accumulation phase on a big portion of your money. There's less time to make mistakes with your money or to experience major volatility now because you will need this money sooner rather than later. Remember, it's not about how much money you *make* but how much you *keep*. The preservation phase is when you will strategically position a portion of your assets to keep them safe, yet continue growing them to outpace inflation for the future and to account for the taxes you will encounter throughout retirement.

Finally, the last phase in the money cycle is *distribution*—distribution to yourself in retirement and to your loved ones upon your passing. Distribution is when you begin to draw from what you've accumulated and preserved and start taking an income from your savings and investments.

CAUTION: DANGER AHEAD!

The biggest mistake most people make is skipping over the preservation phase of the money cycle and going directly from accumulation to distribution.

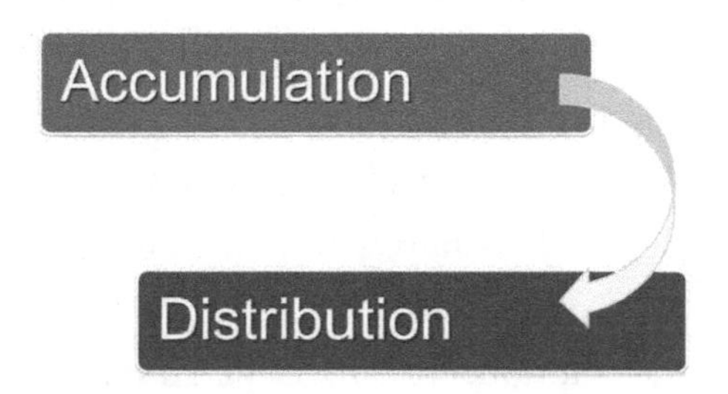

Most people never preserve a portion of their assets to draw from in that all-important first phase of retirement. Instead, they continue to invest all their money as if they were a long way from retirement when it's right around the corner. That's how so many pre-retirees got into trouble back in 2000 and 2008 when the market took nosedives and many investors experienced substantial losses. From September 2000 to September 2003, the market dropped 44.7 percent and took forty-nine months—*more than four years*—to rebound to its previous high. From November 2007 to February 2009, the market dropped 50.9 percent from its previous high and took thirty-seven months to recover. Many investors didn't have time to wait for the market to recover from these corrections, so they panicked and sold as the market was in a decline, realizing the losses in their investments.[3]

---

3 "A History of Bull Markets, Updated," *Morningstar*, data as of March 31, 2015, http://morningstarmag.tumblr.com/post/120535692716/downturns-recoveries-and-expansions-since-1927

The preservation money is essential for financial stability and peace of mind in retirement. When the market has big corrections—as it always has done—and you're forced to take distributions during that time, you're essentially selling your investments for income when the market is down. I call that a "double whammy": withdrawing money for income at the same time your investments are declining. You can never make that money back, and you are depleting your savings much faster than you should. This is how you risk running out of money later in life.

What's the solution? You must be strategic and think in terms of money you will need now, soon, and later. Taking the money cycle into consideration and positioning your assets to preserve money you may need soon helps avoid three common and potentially devastating hazards: market risk, interest rate risk, and sequence of returns risk. Let's explore these in detail.

MARKET RISK

Unfortunately, nobody has a crystal ball when it comes to investing. We have no way of knowing exactly how the market will behave in the future. Several of the worst one-day drops in the history of the stock market are still painfully fresh in our minds, and even though the market recovered to blissful highs after these plunges, many investors who panicked by putting their assets in cash or who withdrew their money because they needed it did not recover.

Market swings of one hundred or more points in either

direction are becoming more common. The last decade has demonstrated major volatility in the form of corrections and outright landslides. That's why the market is a very scary place for money that will be needed during the first stage of retirement (money that will be needed sooner rather than later).

The good news: history shows us that investors who keep their wits and can afford to wait out those kinds of drops in the market still prosper. But what about the rest?

The biggest danger with market risk is for people who need money quickly and cannot wait for a correction to recover, or people who panic when the market dives. These are regular investors just like you and your friends: retirees, people with families, or individuals like Irene who have just lost a spouse. In these cases, people could be forced to sell when the market is down because they need the money for income or because something unexpected happens and they need to access a chunk of money to resolve it. When that happens, they often make bad decisions—decisions that may lead to financial catastrophe. We'll look in depth at how emotions affect investor behavior in chapter 3, but for now just keep in mind that market risk is a major danger for retirees who may or will need to make withdrawals, or who will be forced to take out required minimum distributions (RMDs) from their IRAs once they turn seventy and a half.

INTEREST RATE RISK

According to a 2013 Edward Jones survey, about two-thirds of bond investors have no idea how rising interest rates impact bond values. In fact, most don't know how interest rates impact any of their investments.[4] The truth is that, when interest rates are declining, bond returns tend to be higher. Obviously, that's a good thing for investors. But, as I write this in late 2016, most experts believe that interest rates have dropped just about as low as they can get . . . and that's not a good thing for people holding bonds. *Why? Because bond values typically go down as interest rates rise.*

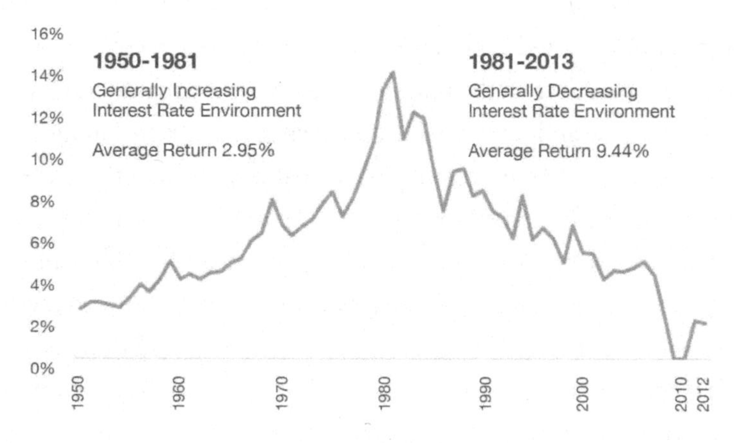

Rates and returns of 10-Year Treasury Bonds. *NYU Stern.*

The concept of rising interest rates corresponding with reduced bond performance can best be illustrated by looking

4 "Nearly Two-Thirds of Americans Are Unaware of How Rising Interest Rates Will Impact Investment Portfolios, Edward Jones Survey Finds," PR Newswire, August 21, 2013, http://www.prnewswire.com/news-releases/nearly-two-thirds-of-americans-are-unaware-of-how-rising-interest-rates-will-impact-investment-portfolios-edward-jones-survey-finds-220497181.html

back at more than half a century of historical performance, as shown in the earlier chart.

As you can see, the period between 1950 and 1981 saw generally increasing interest rates. In 1981, the trend switched to one of mostly declining interest rates. During the period when rates declined, bonds returned a yearly average of 9.44 percent. Nice! But during the period when interest rates increased, bonds saw average returns of only 2.95 percent. Yikes! During those times, people holding bond funds saw periods of significant drops in account balances as well.

During volatile times in the stock market, investors may follow the common wisdom and flee to bonds. However, the general lack of awareness about how interest rates impact bond values poses a serious threat to retirees holding bonds or bond funds. If you are a retiree holding bonds, rising interest rates are particularly dangerous for you because if you need to access the money in your bonds or bond funds quickly, you could be forced to sell at a lower price when the account balance is down.

Since the consensus is that interest rates are likely to increase in the future and potentially trigger a corresponding drop in bond value, retirees would be wise to factor that into their financial plan without delay. Failure to position assets properly—especially when it comes to money that may be needed relatively soon—could spell disaster.

SEQUENCE OF RETURNS RISK

If you've ever heard of dollar cost averaging, then you are somewhat familiar with sequence of returns risk because it is dollar cost averaging's evil twin brother. Sequence of returns risk (or "timing of returns risk") describes risks associated with investing and withdrawing money at a point in time when the balance is down due to investment performance. This hazard can be created because of a combination of market risk, interest rate risk, and a retiree's need for money sooner rather than later. This need is due to three things:

- *Anticipated income needs:* Most commonly, people who are retired must draw out assets as income for their living expenses.
- *Unexpected income or withdrawal needs:* Something unforeseen comes up. Life gets in the way. Perhaps the retiree needs to help a family member or friend, or there's a serious health issue that must be handled.
- *Forced income:* At age seventy and a half, retirees are required to take forced income via RMDs. These are among the most sizeable and reoccurring distributions for retirees, yet often the most overlooked in financial planning. In 2009, the government waived RMDs because the market had dropped significantly in value, but do we really want to trust the government to bail us out if or when it happens again?

As I said, these three reasons for withdrawing money in the near term can affect virtually all retirees to varying degrees. Your portfolio can suffer serious harm because you have to make withdrawals whether you want to or not, regardless of the market conditions at the time. Let's explore how this plays out by considering two investment situations: one during a time of savings and the other during a period of withdrawals.

EXAMPLE 1: ACCUMULATION FOR TEN YEARS WITH NO WITHDRAWALS

The following chart shows what can happen to a $100,000 deposit during a hypothetical ten-year period of savings.

Sequence of Returns Risk

During Accumulation

Deposit: $100,000

10 year average return: 6.00 %

No withdrawals

Ms. Lucky				Mr. Unlucky			
Year	Rate of Return	Annual Gain/Loss	Ending Value	Year	Rate of Return	Annual Gain/Loss	Ending Value
1	30.00%	$30,000	$130,000	1	-30.00%	$-30,000	$70,000
2	20.00%	$26,000	$156,000	2	-20.00%	$-14,000	$56,000
3	10.00%	$15,600	$171,600	3	10.00%	$5,600	$61,600
4	10.00%	$17,160	$188,760	4	10.00%	$6,160	$67,760
5	10.00%	$18,876	$207,636	5	10.00%	$6,776	$74,536
6	10.00%	$20,764	$228,400	6	10.00%	$7,454	$81,989
7	10.00%	$22,840	$251,240	7	10.00%	$8,199	$90,188
8	10.00%	$25,124	$276,364	8	10.00%	$9,019	$99,207
9	-20.00%	$-55,273	$221,091	9	20.00%	$19,841	$119,048
10	-30.00%	$-66,327	$154,764	10	30.00%	$35,715	$154,764

Returns listed are not typical and are for illustration purposes only.

On the left side of the chart (Ms. Lucky's deposit), there was a 30 percent gain the first year, bumping up the balance to $130,000. The second year saw another gain, this time of 20 percent, followed by six straight years of positive returns of 10 percent each. Ms. Lucky closed out her investment cycle with losses of 20 percent and 30 percent in years nine and ten, finishing with a balance of $154,764. This is an example of positive returns early in the savings cycle with a loss at the end.

The opposite happens on the right side of the chart. Mr.

Unlucky took a loss of 30 percent the first year, reducing his $100,000 investment to $70,000. The second year he saw a 20 percent loss, bringing his balance down to $56,000. That was followed by six straight years of positive returns at 10 percent each, and then a positive run-up of 20 percent and 30 percent in years nine and ten. This illustrates an example of negative returns early in the savings cycle with a rebound at the end. Interestingly, Mr. Unlucky's ending balance is the same as Ms. Lucky's: $154,764.

Both investors ended up with the same amount of money regardless of whether the up- and down-years occurred early or late in the investment period. Both experienced a 6 percent average rate of return because the positives and negatives canceled each other out, leaving six years of 10 percent returns (60 percent divided by ten years equals 6 percent). Again, this is during ten years of *savings.* No withdrawals were made during this time.

EXAMPLE 2: DISTRIBUTION FOR TEN YEARS WITH WITHDRAWALS

Now, let's see what happens to these $100,000 deposits during the same hypothetical ten-year period when Ms. Lucky and Mr. Unlucky were making withdrawals for income rather than just saving.

Sequence of Returns Risk

During Distribution

Deposit: $100,000

10 year average return: 6.00 % **Withdrawal rate per year: 6.00 % of initial value ($6k per year)**

Ms. Lucky

Year	Rate of Return	Beginning Value	Withdrawal	Ending Value
		$100,000		
1	30.00%	$130,000	$6,000	$124,000
2	20.00%	$148,800	$6,000	$142,800
3	10.00%	$157,080	$6,000	$151,080
4	10.00%	$166,188	$6,000	$160,188
5	10.00%	$176,207	$6,000	$170,207
6	10.00%	$187,227	$6,000	$181,227
7	10.00%	$199,350	$6,000	$193,350
8	10.00%	$212,685	$6,000	$206,685
9	-20.00%	$165,348	$6,000	$159,348
10	-30.00%	$111,544	$6,000	$105,544

Mr. Unlucky

Year	Rate of Return	Beginning Value	Withdrawal	Ending Value
		$100,000		
1	-30.00%	$70,000	$6,000	$64,000
2	-20.00%	$51,200	$6,000	$45,200
3	10.00%	$49,720	$6,000	$43,720
4	10.00%	$48,092	$6,000	$42,092
5	10.00%	$46,301	$6,000	$40,301
6	10.00%	$44,331	$6,000	$38,331
7	10.00%	$42,164	$6,000	$36,164
8	10.00%	$39,781	$6,000	$33,781
9	20.00%	$40,537	$6,000	$34,537
10	30.00%	$44,898	$6,000	$38,898

Both examples show the same ten-year average rate of return (6 percent) but with a new wrinkle: 6 percent of the initial principal balance is being withdrawn per year for retirement income. For Mr. Unlucky, again there were down years early on but in the late years a rally. The same 10 percent returns existed for the six years in the middle, giving an average return of 6 percent. For Ms. Lucky, the reverse happened—positive years early and then negative years later. But, look at the difference between the ending balances. Even though 6 percent of the initial principal balance was withdrawn per year and experienced the exact same 6 percent average rate of return in both examples, Ms. Lucky finished with $105,544 while Mr. Unlucky had only $38,898!

This is because Ms. Lucky made gains early in the investment cycle on a larger balance and took her losses on a smaller balance. At the end of a period of years when the two investments seemed to average out the same, Mr. Unlucky was left with fewer assets because his losses were taken against the larger balance and the gains were made on the smaller one. Therefore, Mr. Unlucky, with the early drop, ended with a drastically lower balance than Ms. Lucky, *even though they both had the exact same average rate of returns and withdrawals.*

Investors speak a lot about returns, but as these examples show, just knowing the returns is not enough when you depend on your investment for retirement income. Once again, the critical thing to understand is that, although two investments might have the same average returns over time during a period of savings, the sequence of the gains and losses during a period of withdrawals can have as large an impact on a portfolio's ending value as the amount of money invested in the first place.

As you can clearly see, it's not about *returns*. It's about the *account balance* when you're in the distribution phase of retirement.

Remember: the timing of distributions during retirement cannot always be controlled because you may need to withdraw the money sooner rather than later for income, for an unexpected expense, or for forced withdrawals because of RMDs after age seventy and a half.

EXAMPLE 3: COMPOUNDING LOSSES

Here's another way of understanding the effects of sequence of returns risk. It starts with a simple equation:

–30 + 43 = 0

When is minus thirty plus forty-three equal to zero? You might think the answer is "never," but you'd be wrong. When you invest money and lose 30 percent of it, you'll need a 43 percent gain just to get back to zero. Let's say you invest $1 million and you lose 30 percent of it due to a market downturn. How much would you have left? That's easy: $700,000. But, you want to get your balance back to $1 million. What kind of gain would it take to restore your investment to $1 million? Most people would say you'd need a 30 percent gain, but 30 percent of $700,000 is only $210,000, which takes you only to $910,000. *You're going to need a 43 percent gain on your money to recapture the loss from a 30 percent downturn!*

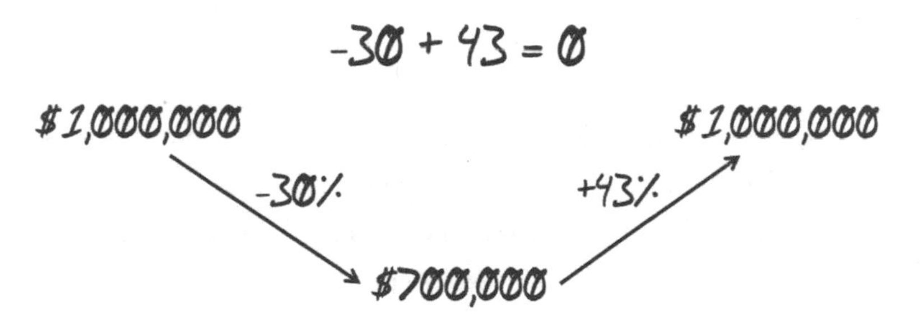

The stock market has gone down almost 50 percent two times since the year 2000, and it's possible that we'll have additional downturns like that in the future. So, let's imagine the very real possibility that you must take not a 30 percent loss but a 50 percent loss on your $1 million investment. How much would you have left now? Half a million, of course. Now, how much must you gain to recapture your loss? Based on the previous example, you might say 60 or 70 percent, but again that would be wrong. *You'll need a 100 percent gain to get back to even.* You will have to double your investment! The more you lose, the harder it is to get your money back.

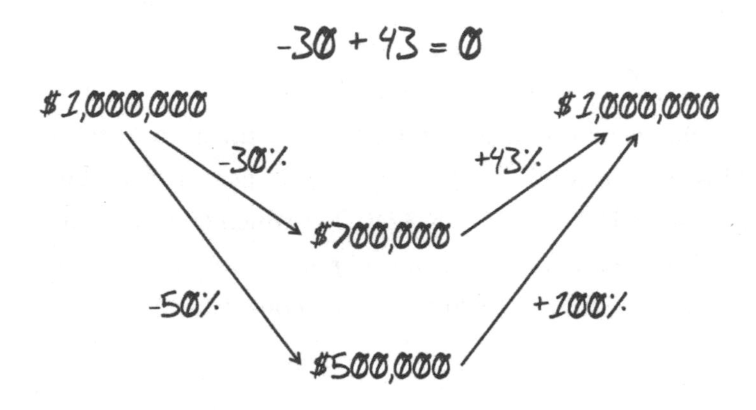

Let's say you are a retiree taking income distributions of 4 percent of the initial balance, and you run into another three-year period of market volatility like we had from 2000 through 2002 when many investors experienced losses of 30, 40, and even 50 percent.

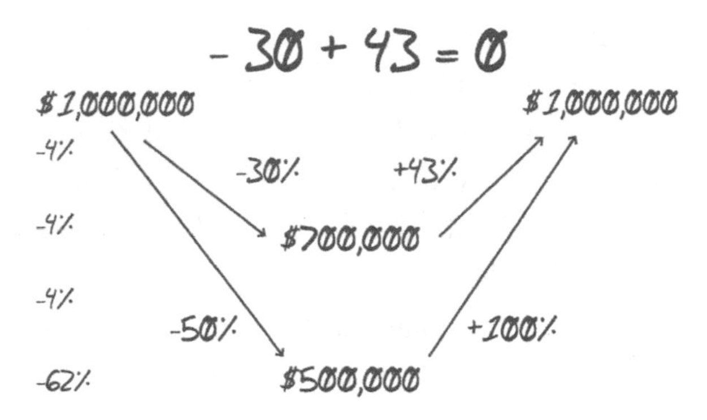

Suddenly, your $1 million principal is reduced not just by 50 percent (which is bad enough!) but by 62 percent or more because you had to take distributions during that period to pay your bills. You'll now need to gain more than 163 percent just to get back to even!

Account Balance versus Rate of Return

Let's recap. In Example 2, Ms. Lucky and Mr. Unlucky both had the same rate of return, yet Ms. Lucky ended up with a lot more money once all was said and done because she took her gains on a larger balance and her losses on a smaller one. The rate of return was irrelevant. Example 3 showed that if one year you suffer a 50 percent loss and the next year you are up 100 percent, you will average a 25 percent rate of return, yet you end up right back where you started. How in the world can you average a 25 percent rate of return but not gain any ground? Well, because success is not measured by rate of return, but by account balance.

I know it's counterintuitive, but lower rates of return *can* result in higher account balances.

This is how it works. This is sequence of returns risk in action: drawing from your money when the balance is down makes it that much harder to recover, which can be devastating when you're in the distribution stage of the money cycle. The market historically has come back, but that takes time—time you may not have as a retiree drawing from your assets. Running out of principal is a very real risk, but you can mitigate that risk by positioning your assets properly. People who structure their investments and withdrawals with an understanding of sequence of returns risk do better than those who don't. The combination of withdrawals and timing can have a huge impact on the value of an investment. This is true of the stock market, and it is also true of the so-called safe haven of bonds. All these vulnerabilities need to be accounted for in your financial plan, and they are accounted for in The Bucket Plan planning process, which we'll explore next.

RECAP

- The money cycle is made up of three distinct phases: accumulation, preservation, and distribution. Many people skip the preservation phase, failing to protect money they may or will need during the early years of their retirement.
- The three biggest dangers facing retirees are market rate risk, interest rate risk, and sequence of returns risk.
- In the distribution stage, it's all about account balances, not rates of return.

Chapter 2

THE BUCKET PLAN® PHILOSOPHY

Buy a Time Horizon, and Invest the Rest!

When I first met with Jerry and Irene to discuss the process of creating their Bucket Plan, they told me the one thing they wanted most in life was peace of mind. They wanted to be able to relax in retirement and have a plan for when the market corrected.

Irene summed up their situation very well for me within the first few minutes of our meeting that day.

"Jerry has always followed the market closely and read the financial news," she said. "It's been his morning ritual for as long as I've known him: bring in the newspaper, grab a cup of coffee, sit down at the kitchen table, and see what the market's been up to. He's always gotten such a kick out of that.

"But it's different now that retirement's right around the corner," she continued with a sigh. "Reading the news is not nearly as much fun for him anymore. He gets so upset when he thinks about how our investments are being affected by all this unpredictability in the economy and in the market."

Jerry nodded in agreement.

"She's right, Jason," he said. "Even when Wall Street's having a solid day, I get totally stressed out imagining what calamity might come tomorrow. I saw what happened to my older brother Ted's retirement savings when the economy tanked in 2008. He was almost wiped out, and he still hasn't fully recovered. Frankly, I'm not sure he ever will. I don't want that to happen to us. We've worked too hard. I don't want to take chances with our retirement. And that's why we called you."

"Well, I'm really happy you did because my team and I have a solution for you," I said. "It's based on a forward-thinking approach to retirement planning called The Bucket Plan® philosophy. One of the most important things I've learned through two decades as a financial planner is the value of the old acronym KISS: Keep It Simple, Soldier. Financial planning can be complicated, even for those of us who are experts in the field. That's why we love The Bucket Plan philosophy for framing out our clients' retirement income and estate plans. It's a super simple yet effective way to understand a complex topic. What it all boils down to is strategically positioning and protecting a portion of your assets to buy yourself a time horizon so you can invest the rest for long-term growth. Here's how it works."

I grabbed a marker and walked over to the giant whiteboard hanging on my office wall. I explained the three phases of the money cycle (accumulation, preservation, and distribution) to Jerry and Irene and told them about the dangers of market risk, interest rate risk, and sequence of returns risk. Then I drew three buckets on the board.

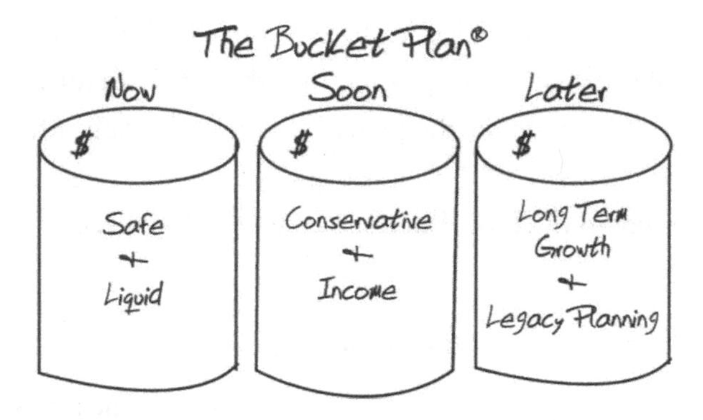

"These three buckets represent our starting place for structuring your assets to provide reliable income throughout retirement. Let's talk about each of them."

THE NOW BUCKET

"Jerry and Irene," I said, "the purpose of the Now bucket is to give you confidence that you have an ample amount of safe and liquid money you can access whenever you need it, as opposed to having to cash in an investment when the market is down. If you have to cash in, you could incur losses, unforeseen taxes, and/or penalties. When you have a fully funded Now bucket, you will never be put into a situation where you need money and don't have enough in the bank. You will always have that feeling of security. When you don't have a properly funded Now bucket, you can become nervous and worried that you won't be able to meet your needs, which can lead to bad decision making and costly mistakes in managing your assets."

Jerry shifted uncomfortably in his chair.

"Simply put, the Now bucket is your cash in the bank," I

continued. "It's not subject to the volatility of the stock market, so it's safer. You're willing to sacrifice the rate of return on this money in exchange for the peace of mind of having it handy."

The money in the Now bucket is set aside for three main things:

- Emergencies or unplanned expenses
- Major planned expenses coming up in the next few years
- Up to one year's income (if you will need it within the next twelve months)

"Unfortunately, emergencies and unplanned expenses happen," I said. "Life just gets in the way sometimes. You have to help a friend or one of your kids, for example, or you or someone close to you experiences a health crisis. When the unexpected strikes and you have a properly funded Now bucket, you won't have to scramble around for money during a time of turmoil. You'll have sufficient cash ready and waiting to help you deal with the inevitable blips and glitches we all face in life."

"How much do people usually put into their emergency fund?" Jerry asked.

"Ah, that's the million-dollar question," I replied. "If there's any trick to setting up the Now bucket, it's figuring out how much to put in there. Not enough and you can't sleep at night because you're worried you won't be able to meet your day-to-day needs or deal with an emergency. Too much and you sacrifice growth on your money. It's like Goldilocks and the three bowls of porridge. You're looking for a balance that is just right.

"Four bad things can happen if you don't have enough

in the Now bucket," I continued. "First, you could be forced to sell investments when they're down, subjecting yourself to sequence of returns risk and locking in losses from which you can't recover. Second, there could be a withdrawal penalty depending on the kind of financial vehicle to which you committed your money. Third, there could be tax consequences on the money you're withdrawing. And fourth, there's the stress that comes from worrying that there might not be enough in the Now bucket to meet your needs."

"Any stress relief you could give us right now would be deeply appreciated," Irene said.

"This whole process is designed to ease your mind, Irene," I replied. "You'll see what I mean as we work our way through it."

Jerry interjected, "I understand why it's bad not to have enough money available for emergencies and unplanned expenses, but I really don't see how it could be wrong to have too much. Better safe than sorry, right?"

"In most cases, that's true, but not necessarily when you're talking about funding your Now bucket," I replied. "There are also four downsides to having too much money in the Now bucket. Number one: it could burn a hole in your pocket. In other words, one or both of you could be tempted to spend that money unnecessarily. Number two, you're sacrificing the growth that you could otherwise earn if you were to invest it. Number three, you're losing purchasing power because the money in your Now bucket is not even making enough to keep up with inflation. And the fourth risk of having too much in the Now bucket is being pestered by the bank investment guys who are always trying to get you to buy something from them."

"I don't like being pressured to do anything, but I really can't stand being pressured to buy something!" Jerry said.

"I hear you, Jerry," I replied. "Just another reason to fund your Now bucket properly. Coming up with the perfect sum isn't terribly difficult; it just requires some thought. Finding the target amount for your upcoming planned expenses is easy. You know how much the tuition payment will be, or how much the new roof will cost. The same is true with your monthly retirement income. You'll know how much money you're going to need each month because we have tools to help us calculate that. It's figuring out the emergency fund that usually gives people the most trouble. Whenever clients struggle with how much to put into their emergency fund, we tell them that the old rule of thumb is *three to six months' worth of living expenses*. However, our goal is to get to whatever magic number gives you the most peace of mind.

Now Bucket	
"Not Enough Money" - If need additional $	"Too Much Money" - If too much lazy $ in bank
1. Forced to sell when market is down 2. Withdrawal penalties 3. Tax consequences 4. Stress	1. Temptation to overspend 2. Sacrificed rate of return 3. Lost purchasing power due to inflation 4. Pressure from the bank to buy something from them

"There's one more important part to funding your Now bucket," I said, "and that's getting buy-in from both of you on the amount of money to set aside for emergencies and unplanned expenses. It's important that you two are on the same page when it comes to your magic number. We want each of you to have total confidence so that you can put your head on the pillow at night and sleep soundly. Achieving that level of mutual assurance can be difficult, especially in households where one spouse has historically made most of the financial decisions, as Jerry has in yours. Often, the other person stays quiet but deep down is not comfortable with the amount his or her spouse has proposed for the Now bucket. When we encourage spouses to talk openly about their feelings, we sometimes find that there was a bigger issue that needed to be addressed, or there was a lack of understanding or education. But in my experience, when both parties participate and speak up, they can work through it.

"Take my clients, Carl and Pearline, as an example," I continued. "These are fictitious names, of course, but the story I'm going to tell you is true. Pearline was the primary decision maker in the family when it came to their finances. The couple had amassed a nest egg of more than $2 million, and we were working through the funding of their Now bucket. Pearline suggested a magic number of $10,000 for their emergency fund. I watched Carl look down and shake his head no when she said that, yet he didn't utter a word. It was clear he wasn't on board with his wife's suggestion, so I asked him to tell me how he felt about it. He confessed that he wasn't comfortable with that figure at all. He didn't understand why she'd want to set aside only $10,000 for emergencies when just about any crisis could wipe that out in a nanosecond."

"I wouldn't be comfortable with that amount either!" Irene exclaimed. "How did they resolve it?"

"Well, I asked Pearline to explain her rationale for wanting a small emergency fund," I replied, "and she said she had a couple of reasons. First, their buying power would go down because that money would be sitting in the bank not even earning enough interest to keep up with inflation. She didn't want to make that kind of sacrifice on a portion of their money. Second, she shared that they had access to a home equity line of $200,000. Pearline knew, if they needed money in a pinch, they could take up to $200,000 out of the equity of their house, which was paid off. Once Carl understood Pearline's thinking, he was completely at ease. If we had never talked it through, he would've always been nervous, believing that $10,000 was all they had available to them in an emergency."

"That makes sense," Irene said. "Jerry and I are good at talking things out, so I'm pretty sure we'll come to a quick agreement when it's time to decide on our magic number."

"I think you will too," I said. "But, while we're on the subject of home equity lines, I want to tell you my thoughts on using them. Some folks are not comfortable keeping even three months' worth of living expenses in their Now bucket because they don't want to lose the opportunity to earn a return on that money. That's fine; in that case, it makes sense to use a home equity line as a backup to a small emergency fund, as Carl and Pearline chose to do. However, I don't recommend using a home equity line for planned expenses or for income because that can get you into big trouble. Planned expenses are just that—planned. You know they're coming, and you know how much they will cost. The same is true for your monthly income needs. If you decide to use your home equity line for income or to fund a planned expense, you must pay interest on it, and eventually you will need to pay that money back somehow. You're just racking up debt for no reason and putting your home in jeopardy." I saw Jerry and Irene exchange uneasy glances.

Clearly, I'd touched a nerve.

"Is there something I need to know about your use of home equity?" I asked.

"Let's talk about that in our next meeting, if you don't mind," Jerry said.

"Fair enough," I said. "So, like I said, it's not a good idea to use home equity for planned expenses or income. But, using it as an emergency fund—or as a backup to a smaller emergency fund—is different. True emergencies are rare. They are the exception to the rule, so if one did crop up, it would be okay if you had to access your home equity line to resolve it. If the stock market is down when it comes time to pay it back, you can make minimum payments while you wait for the rebound, even if that takes a few years. Then, you can shift some money out of your investments and pay it off. Ultimately, your home equity credit should be considered a safety net to be used only in the unlikely event that something weird happens. Accessing it should not become a habit."

Jerry and Irene nodded.

"Back to our discussion of the Now bucket," I said. "In addition to emergencies and unplanned expenses, we all face planned expenses, too, and we'll put money for those in the safe and liquid Now bucket as well. A roof for the house. A kitchen remodel. College tuition payments. A daughter's wedding. A once-in-a-lifetime trip around the world. When you know events like these are coming up in the not-so-distant future, doesn't it make sense to set aside that money now, so you don't have to risk building debt or making withdrawals from your investments when the market is down? Of course it does. With a Now bucket, you can rest assured that the expense is budgeted and fully funded in advance."

"Hey, we were thinking of trading in our old car for a new one within the next few months," Irene said. "We don't want to finance it; we want to buy it outright. Is that the kind of planned expense you're talking about?"

"Yes, that's exactly the sort of thing that belongs in the Now bucket," I said. "And finally, if you are retired or about to retire and will need to draw income from your savings or investments, then we'll put up to twelve months of income into the Now bucket. For example, if we determine that you need to withdraw $2,000 a month in retirement income to supplement your Social Security and pension, we'll put $24,000 into your Now bucket. There's no point in investing that money if you'll need it within the next six months to a year. So, we'll just put it in the Now bucket (the bank) where it will stay safe and sound until you're ready to withdraw it to pay your monthly expenses.

"Does that make sense?"

"Sure does," Jerry said. Irene nodded in agreement.

"Jerry, Irene, I want you to stop and think about the power of the Now bucket for a moment," I said. "Imagine how good it would feel to know that you have a certain amount of money set aside for emergencies, planned expenses, and income while the rest of your money is strategically positioned for preservation and long-term growth. Now, imagine how stressful it is *not* to have that."

"We don't have to imagine it," Irene said. "We're living with that stress right now."

"If it's any consolation, you're not alone," I replied. "Just last week, a woman who came in—I'll call her Nicole—told us the story of just how nerve wracking it can be not to have a Now bucket. Nicole is a widow in her fifties who inherited quite a bit of money from her husband's life insurance policy. She and her two kids, both in their twenties, are living together in the family home. Nicole's kids are always borrowing money from her, and she was afraid that if they saw a pile of easily accessible cash in her checking and savings accounts, they'd be bugging her for even more. Plus, she wanted to continue following her husband's practice of always investing their excess income while otherwise living paycheck to paycheck. So, rather than setting aside money for emergencies and unplanned and planned expenses, Nicole invested all of it, some conservatively, but even more that was growth oriented. And then, sure enough, her son got into trouble and needed to borrow a sum of money fast. We were going through a serious market correction at the time, and even though Nicole had a relatively conservative portfolio, her investments were still down. If she'd had a Now bucket, she could have dealt with her son's emergency without subjecting herself to sequence of returns risk and without locking in those losses. It was a super stressful time for her."

"What a shame," Irene said. "It's too bad she had to learn that lesson the hard way."

"It sure is," I replied. "So, that's the Now bucket in a nutshell: your funding source for emergencies and unplanned expenses, major planned expenses, and retirement income for up to twelve months, if you're retired or retiring soon.

"Basically, it's the short-term income money you need in the bank so you can sleep soundly at night."

"A good night's sleep would be nice, after all this worry over our retirement," Jerry said. "I'll take a Now bucket to go!"

"Well, if you liked the sound of the Now bucket, you're really going to love what comes next: the Soon bucket," I said.

THE SOON BUCKET

I explained to Jerry and Irene that the purpose of the Soon bucket is to provide steady, reliable income when they need it over the next ten years or so.

"I know ten years may not sound very *soon* to you," I said, "but it's a fairly short time frame in the universe of investing. When taken together, the Now and Soon buckets buy you a sufficient time horizon to allow your investments in the Later bucket to grow untouched. You will be confident in your financial plan and be committed to staying the course during market corrections because your Soon bucket is there. This money has minimal or no exposure to market risk, in relation to the stock market; interest rate risk, in relation to bonds; or sequence of returns risk. This is important because, if the market crashes and interest rates start rising—causing your investments to be substantially down—and you don't have a Soon bucket, you may be forced to sell when your balances are low because you need the money to make income withdrawals."

"That's exactly what happened to Jerry's brother Ted when the market crashed in 2008," Irene said. "If he'd had a Soon bucket back then, he might have come out okay."

"No, Irene, he *definitely* would have come out okay," I said, "because the Soon bucket is a more conservative type of money that doesn't experience the volatile trends more common to traditional stock and bond portfolios. The Soon bucket buys you a time horizon and peace of mind so the rest of your money can be invested in the market with an eye toward growth. The Soon bucket is also your inflationary hedge. The prices of everyday items just keep rising with no end in sight. We'll factor that into your plan so you'll be prepared."

I handed Jerry and Irene a slip of paper with the following information:

The Effect of Inflation on Goods and Services Over the Past Twenty-Five Years[5]

- Gasoline per gallon: $1.25 to $2.52
- Milk per gallon: $1.70 to $3.75
- Bread: $1.29 to $2.98
- Postage stamp: $0.25 to $0.49
- Movie tickets: $4.25 to $9.00
- Big Mac: $2.20 to $4.79

"Oh look, Jerry!" Irene said. "The price of your beloved Big Mac has more than doubled over the years. Alas, whatever shall we do?"

---

5 Keene, Jamie (compiler), "Then and Now: How Prices of Goods and Services Have Changed Over the Past 25 Years," *SunSentinel*, August 28, 2015, accessed at http://www.sun-sentinel.com/sfp-then-and-now-how-prices-of-goods-and-services-have-changed-over-the-past-25-years-20150828-story.html on September 15, 2016.

"Don't you worry about that, my dear," Jerry said. "I'll get my weekly burger fix even if I have to sell my plasma to do it."

"Hopefully it won't come to that," I replied. "Your Soon bucket should be a big help there."

"How do you determine how much money to put into this Soon bucket?" Jerry asked.

"An important component of The Bucket Plan planning process is a tool we developed called the Income Gap Assessment, which takes all the guesswork out of funding your Soon bucket," I said. "This analysis provides a formula for discovering how much money you may or will need for income in retirement. If we determine that there is a difference between how much you'll need and how much your pension and/or Social Security will provide, then we'll allocate a portion of your assets to the Soon bucket to make up that difference, plus a little extra to keep up with inflation.

"For example, let's say we conduct the analysis and find that you and Irene will need to draw $20,000 a year from your investments for income to maintain your lifestyle in retirement," I explained. "To achieve our ten-year time horizon, we multiply that $20,000 by ten which totals $200,000. Simple, right? Now that we have your income taken care of for ten years, we next factor in an inflation hedge to ensure you'll be able to keep up with the rising cost of bread, milk, gas, burgers, and the like. We'll set aside 25 percent of your income number—in this example, $50,000—for your inflation hedge. Therefore, your Soon bucket would contain $250,000."

"That makes sense," Irene said. "I like that there's a way to calculate what we'll need rather than just relying on guesswork, hope, and luck."

"Exactly," I said. "If you won't need to draw income from your investments but you are turning seventy and a half within the next ten years, then we'll need to plan for any income you might be forced to take in the form of required minimum distributions (RMDs). We can calculate that amount and strategically position and invest it more conservatively for income in the Soon bucket as well."

I explained that, even if Jerry and Irene would not be drawing from their investments for income or would not be forced to take RMDs within the next ten years, perhaps there was a certain amount of money that they wanted to be more conservative with just in case they needed it.

"Let's face it: no matter how good a job we do as financial planners and no matter how great you are at providing information to us, sometimes life intervenes," I said. "Something happens, and you are laid off from work, or you become disabled, or the kids need help, or an amazing opportunity arises and you need money to capitalize on it above and beyond what is in your Now bucket. If you want to allocate a certain amount of money for these types of events, then we can put it into the Soon bucket where it will be more stable, while it grows until you need it. Keeping a segment of your assets more stable and reliable, that's the purpose of your Soon bucket. You're going to need this money sooner rather than later, so you don't want to be forced to sell or take RMDs when the market is down or when bond values are low. Whatever you do, you don't want to subject this portion of your money to sequence of returns risk."

At this point, I wanted to revisit the subject of sequence of returns risk with Jerry and Irene because understanding this danger was core to their understanding of The Bucket

Plan as the solution. To illustrate, I provided an example of two hypothetical retirees: Mr. Johnson and Ms. Hamilton who both retired at age sixty. They are both taking $8,000 a year in income from their account. They even had the same financial advisor who, based on historical returns, gave them both the same high probability that they would be successful. The only difference between the two was that Mr. Johnson retired in 1969 and Ms. Hamilton retired in 1979.

I showed Jerry and Irene this chart—which, I remind you, represents real market data for these time periods.

	Mr. Johnson Investment: $100,000 Stocks: 60% Bonds: 40% Annual Withdrawal: $8,000 Retired: 1969			Ms. Hamilton Investment: $100,000 Stocks: 60% Bonds: 40% Annual Withdrawal: $8,000 Retired: 1979		
Age	Year	ROR	Year-End Value	Year	ROR	Year-End Value
65	1969	-6.95%	$85,050	1979	11.38%	$103,380
66	1970	8.84%	$84,567	1980	17.85%	$113,828
67	1971	12.45%	$87,093	1981	0.46%	$106,350
68	1972	12.38%	$89,876	1982	25.38%	$125,339
69	1973	-7.12%	$75,475	1983	14.68%	$135,741
70	1974	-14.75%	$56,346	1984	9.18%	$140,204
71	1975	23.64%	$61,666	1985	29.03%	$172,899
72	1976	20.69%	$66,426	1986	20.81%	$200,881
73	1977	-3.67%	$55,987	1987	1.50%	$195,901
74	1978	3.59%	$49,999	1988	13.21%	$213,783
75	1979	11.38%	$47,689	1989	25.96%	$261,286
76	1980	17.85%	$48,200	1990	0.66%	$254,999
77	1981	0.46%	$40,420	1991	24.14%	$308,562
78	1982	25.38%	$42,678	1992	8.24%	$325,991
79	1983	14.68%	$40,944	1993	11.66%	$356,016
80	1984	9.18%	$36,703	1994	-2.42%	$339,404
81	1985	29.03%	$39,357	1995	31.71%	$439,027
82	1986	20.81%	$39,547	1996	14.18%	$493,281
83	1987	1.50%	$32,142	1997	23.84%	$602,868
84	1988	13.21%	$28,388	1998	22.97%	$733,355
85	1989	25.96%	$27,759	1999	9.23%	$793,041
86	1990	0.66%	$19,941	2000	1.24%	$794,898
87	1991	24.14%	$16,755	2001	-4.88%	$748,099
88	1992	8.24%	$10,135	2002	-7.13%	$686,737
89	1993	11.66%	$3,318	2003	17.16%	$796,606
90	1994	-2.42%		2004	8.24%	$854,261
91	1995	31.71%		2005	4.05%	$880,839
92	1996	14.18%		2006	10.15%	$962,262
93	1997	23.84%		2007	7.37%	$1,025,227
94	1998	22.97%		2008	-13.89%	$874,813
	Average ROR 11.78%			Average ROR 11.20%		

Hypothetical clients with data derived from annual returns of the S&P 500 and ten-year Treasury bond for equities and bonds, respectively.

"Mr. Johnson had a thirty-year life expectancy at the time of his retirement, yet as you can see, he was out of money in twenty-four years," I said. "His portfolio was empty. Done. Kaput."

"Ouch. That had to hurt," Jerry said.

"Indeed. But consider Ms. Hamilton, who began her retirement just ten years later with the same portfolio, same advisor, same life expectancy, same everything. Not only was she not out of money in twenty-four years, but at the end of the same thirty-year life expectancy, she had over eight times what she'd started with. It's not that Mr. Johnson had a horrible thirty-year run. His average rate of return over that period was almost 12 percent."

"You'd think he'd be golden, averaging that rate of return and withdrawing only 8 percent," Jerry said.

"Yes, most people—including many traditional financial advisors—would think that," I replied. "In fact, if you're looking at only average returns, Mr. Johnson's portfolio actually outperformed that of Ms. Hamilton, whose average return was 11.2 percent. Yet, she finished with so much more."

"How can that be?" Irene asked.

"Well, first," I replied, "Mr. Johnson wasn't invested for thirty years like Ms. Hamilton because he was out of money in twenty-four. The second interesting thing is that the worst loss he ever experienced was a drop of 14.75 percent. That's it—one time! There were just a few other minor losses in the entire thirty-year period. Now, if I told you just that much, you'd think Mr. Johnson would be fine. Johnson actually had a pretty decent run, but it didn't matter. As this example proves, it's not just about avoiding major losses. It's not about average rate of return. *It's about account balances and the sequence of the returns.* And we're not talking about just squeaking by here. We're talking about the difference between being out of money in twenty-four years or having eight times more than you started with thirty years from now.

"See, that's what the Soon bucket does for you," I continued. "With this bucket, you are conservatively investing the money you may or will need over the next decade so it's not subjected to the whims and dangers of the market, rising interest rates and their corresponding drops in bond value, or sequence of returns risk. You likely won't have sky-high returns with this money, but there will be some growth. Even though we're setting aside ten years' worth of money plus the inflation hedge here, the Soon bucket money may very well last you a good twelve to fifteen years. You'll be able to relax throughout that time, knowing that your needs will be met."

"To recap, the Soon bucket contains the money you will use beyond that first year or so of retirement. We're more conservative with this money because you may need to draw income from it soon if there's a gap between how much money you need to maintain your lifestyle and how much your pension and/or Social Security provide each month. When the market corrects or crashes—not if, but when—you don't want to be forced to pull money out of your long-term investments for income purposes when the market is down. The Soon bucket protects you from having to do that. And, because you're drawing from it during the first phase of retirement, you'll have enough funds to be able to increase your income and keep pace with inflation."

Irene looked at Jerry and smiled. "Do you want to add a Soon bucket to your to-go order?" she asked.

"Yes, please. Make it a double."

I chuckled. Even though designing a financial plan is serious business, I could tell I was going to have fun working with these two.

"Once we've figured out how much money goes into your Soon bucket, we turn to the Later bucket," I said.

THE LATER BUCKET

As I explained to Jerry and Irene, the purpose of the Later bucket is to provide long-term growth and legacy-planning money. Since you've bought a time horizon with the first two buckets, you can confidently commit to investing in the Later bucket without having to worry about day-to-day market volatility. You will also be able to commit to tax and legacy-planning strategies to protect and maximize your estate for your surviving spouse, family members, or other beneficiaries.

"As a general principle, we'll want to develop at least a ten-year time horizon before you access the Later bucket," I explained, "because history shows us that the more time you add to the investment horizon, the more risk you take off the table and the more you increase the odds that the investment will end up producing favorable results. In other words, if you can mentally accept the idea that you won't access the Later bucket funds for ten-plus years, then you should be able to commit to a growth-oriented investment strategy with above-average volatility and potentially achieve very favorable returns. And what's the reason that you can comfortably accept this hands-off approach to your Later bucket money?"

"Because you have enough safe and liquid money in the Now bucket and conservatively invested money in the Soon bucket to meet your shorter-term needs," Irene replied.

"That's right," I said. "All three buckets together give you confidence that you'll achieve substantial growth in your overall portfolios even though you've allocated a portion of your money to more conservative strategies. As I said a moment ago, a lot of people worry that they will not be able to grow as much as they'd like if they put money into that conservative Soon bucket, but the opposite is true. When you know that you have your short-term time horizon taken care of, you can commit to being even more growth oriented in the Later bucket because you are not worried. You know your needs will be met, so there's no reason to touch that other money.

"On the other hand," I continued, "people who don't have a Later bucket tend to invest all their money as if it were Soon-bucket money. They don't dedicate a portion of their overall retirement assets to long-term growth, thereby sacrificing substantial rates of return. And in the end they run out of money, or their surviving spouse runs out of money, all because they invested too conservatively and didn't give their money a chance to go the distance."

"I want to be sure Irene never runs out of money if anything happens to me," Jerry said. "I want to be certain she's taken care of and never has to worry. It'd also be nice if there could be something left over for the kids and grandkids."

"That's what the Later bucket is for, Jerry," I said. "It's your legacy-planning money—not just for your kids but for your surviving spouse. When one spouse passes, the household income almost always goes down. This bucket of money helps you plan for that."

I gave Jerry and Irene the example of a wife getting $2,500 a month in Social Security benefits and her husband receiving $2,000 for a total of $4,500 monthly, or $54,000 annually. When one spouse passes, regardless of which one, the survivor's income will drop substantially. Even if it's the lesser of the two that goes away (in this case, the husband's benefit of $24,000 a year), it's still a massive reduction. Going from $54,000 to $30,000 will make a huge dent in the lifestyle and comfort of the survivor. Not only that, but you also must factor in the loss of any pensions that decrease or end when one spouse passes away.

"And just because there's one less person in the household doesn't mean that all the expenses will necessarily go down too," I said. "Think about it: when one spouse passes, does the mortgage payment go away? Do the real estate taxes go away? Does the gas bill go away? How about the electric bill? The cable bill? The phone bill?"

"Nope, the only thing that goes away is the income," Jerry said.

"Come to think of it, some expenses might even go up for the survivor," Irene mused. "I love to cook, so I've always been the one to do that, but Jerry can't even boil water. If I weren't around, he'd either have to hire someone to cook for him or he'd have to go out, and that costs money. Same with the laundry and all the other things I do around the house. And Jerry mows the lawn, shovels the snow, and does most of the maintenance stuff. If he weren't there, I'd have to pay someone to help me with all that, which is a lot more expensive than doing it ourselves."

"And with life expectancy on the rise, you could conceivably be paying for those things—and everything else—for a very long time," I said. "According to the Social Security Administration, or the SSA, the average life expectancy for a man who is sixty-five years old today is eighty-four; for a woman, it's eighty-seven.[6] Remember, those are averages. The SSA says that 'one out of every four 65-year-olds today will live past age 90.'[7] A renowned researcher, Dr. Robert Pokorski, put together some interesting data about health and long-term care issues affecting this age group, which I think is important for you to understand when considering the purpose of your Later bucket. Take a look."

I handed Jerry and Irene a document with the following statistics:

---

6 Social Security Administration. "Calculators: Life Expectancy," accessed at https://www.ssa.gov/planners/lifeexpectancy.html on September 28, 2016.

7 Ibid.

- More than half (52 percent) of sixty-five-year-olds will need chronic illness care later in life.[8]
- 30 percent of women turning sixty-five by 2019 will require chronic illness care for a minimum of two years and up to five years or more; 21 percent of men will require the same.[9]
- Of every $100 spent on chronic illness care at ages sixty-five and older, $63 is paid out of pocket.[10]
- About one in three people in the lowest income group at age sixty-five will have some of their future chronic illness care expenses paid by Medicaid, compared to only one in twenty in the highest income group. People with higher incomes who eventually qualify for Medicaid are usually individuals who have exhausted their assets after living into their mid- to late-nineties.[11]

"These are shocking numbers," Irene said.

"They are," I replied. "This is why it's critical to strategically plan for these eventualities with the money in the Later bucket. This money is for the second phase of retirement or the

8 Favreault, M. & Dey, Judith, "Long-term Services and Supports for Older Americans: Risks and Financing," ASPE Issue Brief, Department of Health and Human Services (July 1, 2015), p. 3, 9. Accessed at https://aspe.hhs.gov/system/files/pdf/106211 ElderLTCrb-rev.pdf

9 Ibid., Table 1, p. 4.

10 2015 White House Conference on Aging: Final Report (December 29, 2015), p. 5–6. Accessed at https://whitehouseconferenceonaging.gov/2015-WHCOA-Final-Report.pdf

11 Favreault & Dey, Table 6A, p. 8. Accessed at https://aspe.hhs.gov/system/files/pdf/106211/ElderLTCrb-rev.pdf

remainder of your life span in general. It's the money you'll tap into and live on throughout the rest of your life—money that may be handed down or, as these statistics show, money you may need later for major health-care expenses.

"Equally as important, it's the money your surviving spouse will live on for the rest of his or her life," I continued. "Many people don't realize that legacy planning is not just for the kids and grandkids; it's most importantly for the surviving spouse. That's because taxes can be much higher for a single filer, like a widow, than for those who are married-filing-jointly. When one spouse passes away, taxes can go up significantly for the survivor because the standard deduction, which is most people's largest tax deduction, gets cut in half. Poof! Just like that, one of your two personal exemptions also suddenly disappears."

"I don't like that kind of magic trick," Jerry said.

"I don't either. I don't know anyone who does, except maybe the IRS," I replied. "Whereas you might have been in a much lower bracket as a couple, your surviving spouse ends up in a much higher bracket basically overnight. This is a ticking tax time bomb that is poised to go off on your survivor."

I picked up a file folder and handed it to Jerry and Irene.

"Here, I want to show you something. Inside this folder is the tax return of our clients John and Sue," I said. "I've changed their names, of course, but this is a real-world example of what I'm talking about. Unfortunately, Sue passed away in 2014. Let's look at how her death impacted their tax situation."

Jerry and Irene huddled together to study the documents as I explained what they were seeing.

"The Before example is what John and Sue's taxes would

BEFORE

Form **1040** Department of the Treasury - Internal Revenue Service (99) **U.S. Individual Income Tax Return** **2014** OMB No. 1545-0074 IRS Use Only-Do not write or staple in this space.

For the year Jan. 1-Dec. 31, 2014, or other tax year beginning , 2014, ending , 20 — See separate instructions.

Your first name and initial	Last name	Your social security number
John	Frye	112-23-3445
If a joint return, spouse's first name and initial	Last name	Spouse's social security number
Sue	Frye	111-23-4556
Home address (number and street). 36610 Detroit Rd	Apt. no.	Make sure the SSN(s) above and on line 6c are correct.
City, town or post office, state, and ZIP code. If you have a foreign address, also complete spaces below (see instructions). Avon OH 44011		**Presidential Election Campaign** Check here if you, or your spouse if filing jointly, want $3 to go to this fund. Checking a box below will not change your tax or refund. ☐ You ☐ Spouse
Foreign country name	Foreign province/state/county / Foreign postal code	

Filing Status (Check only one box.)
1 ☐ Single
2 ☒ Married filing jointly (even if only one had income)
3 ☐ Married filing separately. Enter spouse's SSN above and full name here. ▶
4 ☐ Head of household (with qualifying person). (See instructions.) If the qualifying person is a child but not your dependent, enter this child's name here. ▶
5 ☐ Qualifying widow(er) with dependent child

Exemptions
6a ☒ **Yourself.** If someone can claim you as a dependent, **do not** check box 6a
b ☒ **Spouse**
Boxes checked on 6a and 6b: 2
No. of children on 6c who: • lived with you • did not live with you due to divorce or separation (see instructions)
Dependents on 6c not entered above

c Dependents: (1) First name Last name	(2) Dependent's social security number	(3) Dependent's relationship to you	(4) Chk if child under age 17 qualifying for child tax credit (see instructions)
			☐
			☐
			☐
			☐

If more than four dependents, see instructions and check here ▶ ☐

d Total number of exemptions claimed — Add numbers on lines above ▶ 2

Income

Attach Form(s) W-2 here. Also attach Forms W-2G and 1099-R if tax was withheld.

If you did not get a W-2, see instructions.

7	Wages, salaries, tips, etc. Attach Form(s) W-2	7	5,000
8a	**Taxable** interest. Attach Schedule B if required	8a	2,345
b	**Tax-exempt** interest. **Do not** include on line 8a — 8b		
9a	Ordinary dividends. Attach Schedule B if required	9a	250
b	Qualified dividends — 9b 250		
10	Taxable refunds, credits, or offsets of state and local income taxes	10	
11	Alimony received	11	
12	Business income or (loss). Attach Schedule C or C-EZ	12	
13	Capital gain or (loss). Attach Schedule D if required. If not required, check here ▶ ☐	13	
14	Other gains or (losses). Attach Form 4797	14	
15a	IRA distributions 15a — b Taxable amount	15b	15,500
16a	Pensions and annuities 16a — b Taxable amount	16b	23,450
17	Rental real estate, royalties, partnerships, S corporations, trusts, etc. Attach Schedule E	17	
18	Farm income or (loss). Attach Schedule F	18	
19	Unemployment compensation	19	
20a	Social security benefits 20a 34,525 — b Taxable amount	20b	22,837
21	Other income	21	
22	Combine the amounts in the far right column for lines 7 through 21. This is your **total income** ▶	22	69,382

Adjusted Gross Income

23	Educator expenses	23	
24	Certain business expenses of reservists, performing artists, and fee-basis government officials. Attach Form 2106 or 2106-EZ	24	
25	Health savings account deduction. Attach Form 8889	25	
26	Moving expenses. Attach Form 3903	26	
27	Deductible part of self-employment tax. Attach Schedule SE	27	
28	Self-employed SEP, SIMPLE, and qualified plans	28	
29	Self-employed health insurance deduction	29	
30	Penalty on early withdrawal of savings	30	
31a	Alimony paid b Recipient's SSN ▶	31a	
32	IRA deduction	32	
33	Student loan interest deduction	33	
34	Tuition and fees. Attach Form 8917	34	
35	Domestic production activities deduction. Attach Form 8903	35	
36	Add lines 23 through 35	36	
37	Subtract line 36 from line 22. This is your **adjusted gross income** ▶	37	69,382

For Disclosure, Privacy Act, and Paperwork Reduction Act Notice, see separate instructions. Form **1040** (2014)
EEA

have been had Sue not passed away that year. The After example represents what actually happened to their taxes following her death."

AFTER

Exemptions

6a	X Yourself. If someone can claim you as a dependent, do not check box 6a				Boxes checked on 6a and 6b: 1
b	Spouse				No. of children on 6c who: • lived with you ___ • did not live with you due to divorce or separation (see instructions) ___
c	Dependents: (1) First name / Last name	(2) Dependent's social security number	(3) Dependent's relationship to you	(4) Chk if child under age 17 qualifying for child tax credit (see instructions)	Dependents on 6c not entered above ___
	If more than four dependents, see instructions and check here ▶				Add numbers on lines above ▶ 1
d	Total number of exemptions claimed				

Income

Attach Form(s) W-2 here. Also attach Forms W-2G and 1099-R if tax was withheld.

If you did not get a W-2, see instructions.

Line	Description	Sub-box	Sub-amount	Line	Amount
7	Wages, salaries, tips, etc. Attach Form(s) W-2			7	
8a	Taxable interest. Attach Schedule B if required			8a	2,345
b	Tax-exempt interest. Do not include on line 8a	8b			
9a	Ordinary dividends. Attach Schedule B if required			9a	250
b	Qualified dividends	9b	250		
10	Taxable refunds, credits, or offsets of state and local income taxes			10	
11	Alimony received			11	
12	Business income or (loss). Attach Schedule C or C-EZ			12	
13	Capital gain or (loss). Attach Schedule D if required. If not required, check here ▶ ☐			13	
14	Other gains or (losses). Attach Form 4797			14	
15a	IRA distributions	15a		15b	15,500
	b Taxable amount				
16a	Pensions and annuities	16a		16b	23,450
	b Taxable amount				
17	Rental real estate, royalties, partnerships, S corporations, trusts, etc. Attach Schedule E			17	
18	Farm income or (loss). Attach Schedule F			18	
19	Unemployment compensation			19	
20a	Social security benefits	20a	21,075	20b	17,914
	b Taxable amount				
21	Other income			21	
22	Combine the amounts in the far right column for lines 7 through 21. This is your **total income** ▶			22	59,459

Adjusted Gross Income

Line	Description	Sub-box	Sub-amount	Line	Amount
23	Educator expenses	23			
24	Certain business expenses of reservists, performing artists, and fee-basis government officials. Attach Form 2106 or 2106-EZ	24			
25	Health savings account deduction. Attach Form 8889	25			
26	Moving expenses. Attach Form 3903	26			
27	Deductible part of self-employment tax. Attach Schedule SE	27			
28	Self-employed SEP, SIMPLE, and qualified plans	28			
29	Self-employed health insurance deduction	29			
30	Penalty on early withdrawal of savings	30			
31a	Alimony paid b Recipient's SSN ▶	31a			
32	IRA deduction	32			
33	Student loan interest deduction	33			
34	Tuition and fees. Attach Form 8917	34			
35	Domestic production activities deduction. Attach Form 8903	35			
36	Add lines 23 through 35			36	
37	Subtract line 36 from line 22. This is your **adjusted gross income** ▶			37	59,459

For Disclosure, Privacy Act, and Paperwork Reduction Act Notice, see separate instructions. Form 1040 (2015)

EEA

"Let's compare the two returns. Line 8a stayed the same; this is typically interest income from money in the bank. Line 9a stayed the same; this is typically dividend income from investments. John and Sue were living off their IRA distributions—see here, at line 15b on the tax return—so that also stayed the same.

The pension amount on line 16b stayed the same; although, that's not always the case following a spouse's passing. But, because of Sue's death, Social Security income on line 20a went down from $34,525 to $21,075. That's a more than a $13,000 drop. This, combined with the $5,000 no longer received from Sue's part-time job really had an effect. The income fell by more than $18,000 for the surviving spouse."

"Wow," said Jerry, shaking his head. "Seeing this gives me an idea. I think we should print tax returns on facial tissues because we're all paying through the nose."

"Jerry, if you think that's bad, wait until you see the back of John and Sue's return."

BEFORE (BACK)

Tax and Credits	38	Amount from line 37 (adjusted gross income)	38	69,382
	39a	Check if: { [X] **You** were born before January 2, 1950, [ ] Blind. [X] **Spouse** was born before January 2, 1950, [ ] Blind. } **Total boxes checked** ▶ 39a [2]		
	b	If your spouse itemizes on a separate return or you were a dual-status alien, check here ▶ 39b [ ]		
Standard Deduction for -	40	**Itemized deductions** (from Schedule A) **or** your **standard deduction** (see left margin)	40	14,800
	41	Subtract line 40 from line 38	41	54,582
• People who check any box on line 39a or 39b **or** who can be claimed as a dependent, see instructions.	42	**Exemptions.** If line 38 is $152,525 or less, multiply $3,950 by the number on line 6d. Otherwise, see instructions	42	7,900
	43	**Taxable income.** Subtract line 42 from line 41. If line 42 is more than line 41, enter -0-	43	46,682
	44	**Tax** (see instructions). Check if any from: **a** [ ] Form(s) 8814 **b** [ ] Form 4972 **c** [ ]	44	6,056
	45	**Alternative minimum tax** (see instructions). Attach Form 6251	45	
	46	Excess advance premium tax credit repayment. Attach Form 8962	46	
	47	Add lines 44, 45, and 46 ▶	47	6,056
• All others:	48	Foreign tax credit. Attach Form 1116 if required	48	

Other Taxes	57	Self-employment tax. Attach Schedule SE	57	
	58	Unreported social security and Medicare tax from Form: **a** [ ] 4137 **b** [ ] 8919	58	
	59	Additional tax on IRAs, other qualified retirement plans, etc. Attach Form 5329 if required	59	
	60 a	Household employment taxes from Schedule H	60a	
	b	First-time homebuyer credit repayment. Attach Form 5405 if required	60b	
	61	Health care: individual responsibility (see instructions) Full-year coverage [ ]	61	
	62	Taxes from: **a** [ ] Form 8959 **b** [ ] Form 8960 **c** [ ] Instructions; enter code(s)	62	
	63	Add lines 56 through 62. This is your **total tax** ▶	63	6,056

AFTER (BACK)

Tax and Credits	38	Amount from line 37 (adjusted gross income)	38	59,459
	39a	Check if: [X] You were born before January 2, 1951, [ ] Blind. [ ] Spouse was born before January 2, 1951, [ ] Blind. **Total boxes checked** ▶ **39a** [1]		
	b	If your spouse itemizes on a separate return or you were a dual-status alien, check here ▶ **39b** [ ]		
Standard Deduction for -	40	**Itemized deductions** (from Schedule A) **or** your **standard deduction** (see left margin)	40	7,850
• People who check any box on line 39a or 39b **or** who can be claimed as a dependent, see instructions.	41	Subtract line 40 from line 38	41	51,609
• All others:	42	**Exemptions.** If line 38 is 154,950 or less, multiply 4,000 by the number on line 6d. Otherwise, see instructions	42	4,000
	43	**Taxable income.** Subtract line 42 from line 41. If line 42 is more than line 41, enter -0-	43	47,609
	44	**Tax** (see instructions). Check if any from: **a** [ ] Form(s) 8814 **b** [ ] Form 4972 **c** [ ]	44	7,676
	45	**Alternative minimum tax** (see instructions). Attach Form 6251	45	
	46	Excess advance premium tax credit repayment. Attach Form 8962	46	
	47	Add lines 44, 45, and 46 ▶	47	7,676

Other Taxes	57	Self-employment tax. Attach Schedule SE	57	
	58	Unreported social security and Medicare tax from Form: **a** [ ] 4137 **b** [ ] 8919	58	
	59	Additional tax on IRAs, other qualified retirement plans, etc. Attach Form 5329 if required	59	
	60 a	Household employment taxes from Schedule H	60a	
	b	First-time homebuyer credit repayment. Attach Form 5405 if required	60b	
	61	Health care: individual responsibility (see instructions) Full-year coverage [X]	61	
	62	Taxes from: **a** [ ] Form 8959 **b** [ ] Form 8960 **c** [ ] Instructions; enter code(s)	62	
	63	Add lines 56 through 62. This is your **total tax** ▶	63	7,676

"Look at line 40. The standard deduction—John and Sue's biggest tax deduction—was cut in half following Sue's passing. The personal exemption on line 42 was, again, cut in half for the survivor. And now, check out line 63, the total amount of tax dollars owed. This is the bottom line, the ticking tax time bomb. John's income dropped by $18,000 that year, yet his tax liability increased by $1,620!"

"Oh, my gosh! That doesn't seem fair," Irene said. "No, it doesn't, but that's the way it is. Income goes down, taxes go up, and the survivor is caught in the crosshairs.

"But here's the good news, guys," I continued. "If you're a retiree with a Bucket Plan, it will address events like this because they are factored into your plan. And since the Now and Soon buckets have bought you a healthy time horizon, you can feel comfortable making investments for growth and legacy planning for your spouse or family in the Later bucket. So when the market fluctuates as it does from time to time, you're not so concerned about it. You're confident that your surviving spouse will be okay because your Later bucket is there for growth, not only to provide needed income in the future but also to anticipate and defuse the tax time bomb when one of you passes away. Setting up a Bucket Plan boils down to using your assets, however much you have, to properly fund the buckets based on your unique situation, and ensuring we have chosen the best portfolios and products to fit the objectives of each of your buckets."

"But, Jason, I have a question," Irene said. "The Soon bucket money is going to run out at some point, right? What happens then?"

"You'll reload it," I replied. "You'll buy another time horizon by repositioning a sum of money from your Later bucket, which by then will have been allowed to grow untouched for several years. We'll start looking at that about five years before your Soon bucket should be exhausted. If the market has had a good run and is at a high at that time, then we may take some earnings off the table right then and there and reload your Soon bucket. But let's say the opposite is true and the market just had a big correction. Because you still have five years of income left in the Soon bucket, you have time to wait for the market to rebound before we take some earnings off the table and reload it."

"That makes sense," Irene said. "I really love how this process factors in all sorts of contingencies. It seems as if there's a solution for just about everything."

The Bucket Plan Benefits

At that moment, our receptionist tapped on the door and offered us coffee and a basket of freshly baked chocolate chip cookies. As we enjoyed our snack, I continued my explanation of The Bucket Plan philosophy and planning process.

"The Bucket Plan planning process has many benefits in addition to being an effective way to position assets for a secure retirement," I said. "First, it's *educational.* Going through this process with a highly skilled holistic financial planner is like receiving a minidegree in finance. You'll learn about every aspect of your financial life. You'll also learn a lot about yourself, your spouse, and your thoughts and feelings about money—that may have been holding you back in the past. If you think financial planning is boring, think again. Our clients—from the most financially savvy to the least financially knowledgeable—thoroughly enjoy the learning process and come away feeling much more confident and better equipped to face the future."

"I already feel better, Jason, and we haven't even started building our Bucket Plan yet," Irene said with a smile. "I can tell I'm going to learn a lot by going through this process with you. I'm really excited about it. I've never been that involved with our finances. I just let Jerry handle it because he likes it so much."

"That's very typical," I said. "Most couples operate the same way. One spouse naturally assumes the financial role, not because he or she is more capable but because that person simply enjoys it more or just took on the responsibility."

"I had no idea you wanted to be involved, Irene," Jerry said. "That's why I always dealt with our finances myself. It's nice to know we'll be able to talk about this and handle it together from now on. Hopefully that'll calm me down a little."

"Jerry, that's another positive thing about The Bucket Plan planning process," I said. "Going through this process will definitely ease your mind because it's a tailored approach based on *your personal comfort level* for volatility and risk in each bucket. The Bucket Plan is not a one-size-fits-all proposition. Your unique financial situation; your personal risk tolerance; your hopes and dreams, and strengths and challenges all are methodically assessed and taken into consideration as the plan is being built.

"Another great thing about the process is that it provides a *big-picture view* of your finances—a view you just can't get any other way," I continued. "The plan allows you to see your entire macrofinancial landscape rather than a disjointed microperspective of 'this investment' or 'that insurance policy,' and you can observe how everything fits together in a comprehensive way. Your Bucket Plan also gives you *a solid foundation* on which to grow. You'll be able to see the stability built into your plan—the stability you need to fully enjoy your retirement with confidence.

"Most important, your Bucket Plan mitigates *sequence of returns risk*. As you've already learned from your brother Ted's unfortunate situation, one of the biggest dangers in retirement is being forced to draw income from your investments when your account balances are down because, in many cases, it's impossible to get back what you lost. Consequently, you risk running out of money before you run out of years. Your Bucket Plan addresses that risk.

"But there's another terrific thing that The Bucket Plan does for retirees, and it deals with the psychology of investing," I said. "I'm sending you two home with a white paper my team and I wrote about a relatively new field of study called 'behavioral finance' or 'behavioral investing.' It's quite an interesting subject. I'd like for you to read this before our next meeting in two weeks."

As I pulled the folder containing the white paper from my desk drawer, Irene stood and extended her hand.

"I'll take custody of that document, Professor," she said, "and I'll make certain our homework is complete in time for our next class session."

RECAP

- The Bucket Plan planning process is educational and customizable.
- The Now bucket is your safe and liquid money in the bank for emergencies, unplanned expenses, major planned expenses, and income for up to twelve months, if needed.
- The purpose of the Soon bucket is to provide steady, reliable income and an inflation hedge over the next ten or so years. It is conservatively invested to protect assets from the dangers of market risk, interest rate risk, and sequence of returns risk.
- The Now and Soon buckets buy you a time horizon so you can confidently invest the rest of your assets for long-term growth in the Later bucket.
- Legacy planning is not just for the kids but most importantly for the surviving spouse.

Chapter 3

BEHAVIORAL FINANCE AND INVESTMENTS

The Worst Behavioral Mistakes Investors and Advisors Make . . . and How to Avoid Making Them

Here's the white paper I sent home with Jerry and Irene that day . . .

BEHAVIORAL FINANCE AND INVESTMENTS

No one can forecast the future, and that's why the stock market is such a scary place for money that will be needed during the first stage of retirement. It's terrifying to think that the nest egg you worked so hard to accumulate can be wiped out due to unpredictable market risk, interest rate risk, and sequence of returns risk. As bad as these dangers are on their own, they can be compounded even further by your and your advisor's emotions and behavior.

Most traditional financial planners use academic theory as the basis for the plans they build. Most notably, Modern Portfolio Theory, developed by Dr. Harry Markowitz in 1952, has guided investors and those who advise them on how to structure a portfolio with the goal of maximizing return with the least amount of risk. While Markowitz's theory is still relevant and widely used, it has a major gap: it assumes people are rational.

We've learned a lot since 1952, including the fact that when it comes to investing, people are *not* always rational. Investors and their advisors think they can "beat" the market, but they often end up buying high and selling low. They panic during times of volatility, selling off their holdings and taking losses, and then sitting on the sidelines missing the recovery. Bad surprises (like a falling market) impact retirees more than good surprises (like a climbing market) because people tend to sell investments on the way down but don't buy in again until the market has recovered. There is a lopsided nature to gains and losses. Most retirees lump their investments together without separating the money they may need for income sooner rather than later from the money they can dedicate to a longer-term investment timeline.

For all these reasons, the relatively new field of behavioral finance seeks to combine behavioral and cognitive psychological theory with conventional economics and finance to explain why people make irrational financial decisions. This white paper discusses the biggest behavioral mistakes we see investors and their advisors make and provides insight into how you can potentially avoid making them.

Behavior 1: Many investors and advisors think they can "beat" the market, but end up buying high and selling low—which is the opposite of what you want to do with your retirement money.

The financial market is made up of millions of participants, many of them just like you. They are buyers and sellers who voluntarily agree to trade shares of companies all over the world. Each day, tens of millions of trades take place in the world's stock markets. The collective knowledge of those participants is powerful. Together, we know more than we do alone. Think of the stock market as a large information-processing machine. All this information affects the price of stocks. No one can really know if that price is right, but thanks to the market's processing power, we can treat the price as the best estimate of the stock's value. Stock prices are like any other prices; they move up and down based on new information, and they do so very quickly based on the market participants' reactions to the latest information.

Many advisors believe they need to be able to predict where prices are going to get their clients ahead, but this belief is not necessarily correct. Trying to predict the movements of the financial markets only adds anxiety and creates unnecessary risk to long-term investments, and often results in less-than-ideal outcomes.

This phenomenon is well-illustrated by a 2002 study by Barber and Odean[12] in which the researchers sorted households

---

12 Barber, B. M. and Odean, T., "Trading Is Hazardous to Your Wealth: The Common Stock Investment Performance of Individual Investors," *Journal of Finance*, 55, (2000), p. 773–806. Accessed at http://faculty.haas.berkeley.edu/odean/papers%20current%20versions/individual_investor_performance_final.pdf

into groups based on their monthly trading activity from 1991 to 1996. This was one of the greatest growth periods in the history of the stock market. The total sample consisted of approximately 65,000 investors. The 20 percent of those investors who traded most actively from 1991 to 1996 earned an annual net return of 11.4 percent. Not bad. Most people would be happy with that rate of return. But the buy-and-hold investors (the 20 percent who traded least actively during those five years) earned 18.5 percent net of costs.

That seven-percentage point spread doesn't sound like much until you do the math. Consider what would have happened to an investment of $100,000 during that period. An active trader with an annual net return of 11.4 percent on his $100,000 investment would have finished the five-year period with $170,157. Yet his buy-and-hold neighbor would have walked away with $230,366. That's roughly over $60,000 more!

Investors who stay the course and let the market do its thing consistently do better than those who try to out-guess and outmaneuver the system. And that's why having a Bucket Plan is so important. When you set up Now and Soon buckets, you buy yourself a time horizon to let your Later bucket money sit and grow untouched. But when you don't have Now and Soon buckets and you hear the financial channel pundits screaming that the sky is falling because of market volatility, it can influence you or your advisor to take evasive action. When you get nervous and start changing and reallocating investments within your portfolio, you will not do as well. That's a scientific fact, as evidenced by the Barber and Odean study.

If your plan hasn't changed, don't change your portfolio!

That was an example of what can happen during a five-year period of historic growth. Now let's look at the other end of the spectrum: the reality of what most people earn on their money during a more typical investment phase. This chart, put together by BlackRock, illustrates how the average investor did compared to various investment classes such as stocks (S&P 500), bonds, gold, oil, international stocks, and home sales during the twenty-one-year period of 1995 to 2015. The "average investor" was defined by analyzing mutual fund sales, redemptions, and exchanges every month during the twenty-one-year period to arrive at a snapshot of investor behavior.

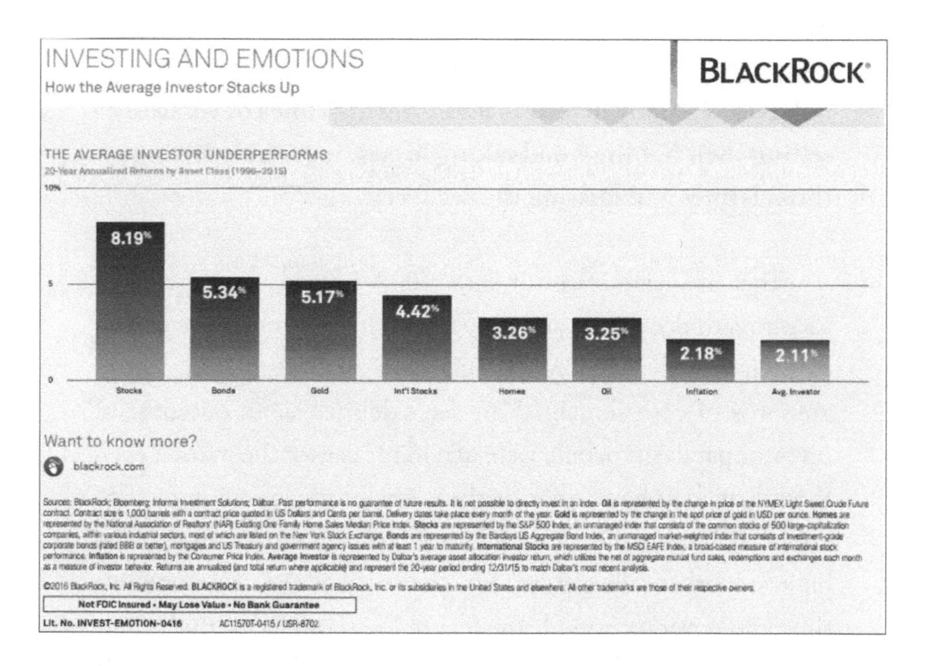

As you can see, the average investor's rate of return of 2.11 percent (the final bar) is less than that of the other classes; in the case of stocks, it's substantially less. Not only that, but the average investor didn't even earn enough to outpace inflation.

This is the unfortunate reality. When the average investor and/or their advisor tries to predict the market, they're competing against the collective knowledge of millions of other buyers and sellers. That kind of guessing game is not stacked in your favor. A better approach is to harness that collective wisdom and let the markets work for you over the long term. Having a Bucket Plan in place allows you to do that in the Later bucket with confidence.

Behavior 2: Many investors panic during times of volatility, selling their holdings and taking losses, inevitably sitting on the sidelines and missing the recovery.

The financial crisis of late 2008 caused panic-stricken investors to flee stocks and move to cash . . . often at the urging of their equally panicky financial advisors. Years later, record amounts of cash remained on the sidelines as an outcome of investor paralysis: people were afraid to reenter the market even though it may have been in their long-term best interests to do so. Consequently, those investors missed out on one of the biggest market rallies in history. They sold at the worst possible time and never recovered. The fear of loss, coupled with the tendency to procrastinate, causes this behavior to be catastrophic to an investor's long-term financial plan. The media fuels this behavior. During times of volatility, the media makes people and their advisors even more fearful, shouting that there is no end in sight and that the markets are melting down. In times of prosperity, they make predictions of funds or investments viewers need to buy, such as the next hot tech stock or mutual fund. By sheer luck, some of these predictions might pay off, but they seem to do more harm than good for the individual investor.

Behavior 3: Many investors and advisors let the possibility of bad surprises impact them more than the potential for good ones.

Over fifty years ago, Nobel Laureate Paul Samuelson offered one of his MIT colleagues a bet on a coin flip during lunch.[13] If the colleague chose heads and the coin landed on heads, he would win $200. But if he called heads and the coin landed on tails, he would lose $100. Samuelson's colleague rejected the bet. But why? Would you have gambled your money or declined?

Samuelson's colleague offered the following reason for rejecting the bet: "I won't bet because I would feel the $100 loss more than the $200 gain." If you would have rejected the bet also, you probably felt the same way. Studies on the human mind reveal that most individuals hate to lose more than they like to gain. In a later study, Nobel Laureate Daniel Kahneman and his long-time collaborator Amos Tversky estimated that,

---

13 Samuelson, Paul A., "Risk and Uncertainty: A Fallacy of Large Numbers," *Scientia*, 98.612, (1963), p. 108–113. Accessed at https://www.casact.org/pubs/forum/94sforum/94sf049.pdf

on average, losses loom about two to two-and-a-half times longer than gains.[14]

So, how does this relate to real life? Jose and Wanda, a sixty-five-year old couple, are getting ready to retire and have built up a nice nest egg. That nest egg must supplement their fixed income through retirement, which, based on today's life expectancy per the National Institutes of Health, means there is a 50 percent chance at least one of them will live to age ninety. For Jose and Wanda, the losses they experienced in 2008 still loom over them, and although they didn't panic and sell at the time, they feel at this point in their lives that achieving larger gains isn't worth the losses they could experience (just like in the coin flip game). So, they consider moving all their money into low-yielding fixed investments at the bank. While this approach is certainly conservative and they won't experience losses, they also run the risk of running out of money because the bank yields aren't even enough to keep up with inflation. They'll have no long-term money growing in the market to help offset the rising cost of living ten, twenty, or even thirty years down the road. We have seen this loss aversion make clients invest too conservatively, which ultimately means their nest egg cannot keep up with the rising cost of living. The good news for Jose and Wanda is that they will have a Bucket Plan in place going forward, with growth-focused money in their Later bucket and with

---

14 Kahneman, Daniel and Tversky, Amos, "Prospect Theory: An Analysis of Decision Under Risk," *Econometrica: Journal of the Econometric Society*, 47.2, (1979), p. 263–291. Accessed at https://www.princeton.edu/~kahneman/docs/Publications/prospect_theory.pdf

stability and peace of mind in their Soon bucket. By structuring their money in this way, the possibility of not keeping up with inflation won't even be a blip on their radar.

Behavior 4: Many investors lump their investments together without separating the money they may need for income soon from the money they can dedicate to a longer-term time commitment.

If you're like many investors, the largest account value you will have accumulated will be in your retirement plan account(s), such as your pension, 401(k), 403(b), or IRAs. During your working years, you attempt to sock away as much as you can into these vehicles each year, knowing you will need this money to live on during retirement. Let's assume you and your spouse are now looking to retire. The two of you have spent the last few decades saving in your retirement plan and have amassed $800,000. When you separate from employment, you roll those 401(k) assets into IRAs and invest it in a portfolio made up of 60 percent stocks/equities and 40 percent bonds/fixed income. Since you need to supplement your Social Security income, you begin to withdraw four percent per year out of your $800,000 investment to live on (which gives you $32,000 annually), and you plan to increase that amount by 3 percent each year to keep up with inflation. You think, *as long as I can average more than four percent return, I should never run out of money.*

This is one of the biggest mistakes we see investors and retirees make. They don't account for sequence of returns risk. Sequence of returns risk is the impact that the timing of returns can have on your account balance. In its most simplistic form, if you experience larger negative returns early while you are withdrawing income, you will deplete your account balance at a much greater rate.

But with The Bucket Plan® approach to allocating your assets, you mitigate the potential for sequence of returns risk on money you may or will need to access during the early stages of retirement. Within The Bucket Plan, each bucket has a purpose to mitigate risks and to help you avoid making bad decisions that could hurt your long-term plan.

BIGGEST BEHAVIORAL MISTAKES INVESTORS MAKE

- **Behavior 1:** Trying to "beat" the market but instead ending up buying high and selling low—the opposite of what you want to do with your retirement money.
- **Behavior 2:** Panicking during times of volatility, selling your holdings and taking losses, and then sitting on the sidelines and missing the recovery.
- **Behavior 3:** Letting the possibility of bad surprises impact you more than the potential for good ones.
- **Behavior 4:** Lumping your investments together without separating the money you may soon need for income from the money you can dedicate to a longer-term time commitment.

The Soon bucket eliminates the potential for Behaviors 2, 3, and 4. The Later bucket eliminates the potential for Behavior

1 because you now become a rational investor who lets capital markets work for you rather than competing against them.

And that's why The Bucket Plan philosophy is so important. It not only enables you to build a financial plan and eliminate those dangers we've talked about in this white paper, but it also allows you to sleep soundly at night. Having a Bucket Plan with a Soon bucket established (which contains a much more conservative alternative to the traditional stock and bond portfolio) gives you that kind of peace of mind. Consequently, it prevents a lot of the panic and poor decision making that can occur during times of market volatility.

Chapter 4

THE ASSET SHEET QUESTIONNAIRE

Identifying and Documenting Assets and Liabilities

The day after my initial meeting with Jerry and Irene, my receptionist, Linda, handed me this message slip when I returned from lunch:

Important Message

To: *Jason*

Date: *Oct 7* Time: *2:33p*

From: *Jerry*

Telephoned	*X*	Please Call	*X*
Came By		**Rush**	*X*
Needs Appt.	*X*	Will Call	

Message:

Jerry and Irene don't want to wait two weeks to start Bucket Plan. Need appointment ASAP!

They must have read their homework assignment! I thought with a smile as I walked down the hall to my office. Once people understand the power of The Bucket Plan® in mitigating risk and growing their money for the future, they often don't want to let another day go by without getting one of their own.

I buzzed Linda's desk. "Linda, when's my next available opening?"

"Looks like next Tuesday afternoon."

"Okay, let's see if they can make that work. Give them a call and let them know."

The Process Continues

On Tuesday, Jerry and Irene were right on time for our appointment. After taking our places at the table and engaging in some small talk—which was always entertaining when Jerry was around—we got down to business.

"Now that you've decided to engage with us to create your own customized Bucket Plan, we'll continue the planning process," I said. "It contains all the elements necessary to understand your financial situation and put a plan in place. The process is made up of six key components:

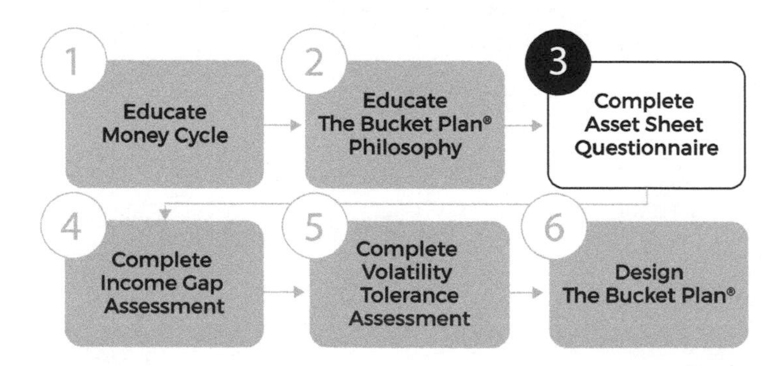

"We've already covered the first two components—the money cycle (accumulation, preservation, and distribution) and The Bucket Plan philosophy—in our previous meeting. The next step in the process utilizes one of the most important tools we have for creating a sound retirement plan: the Asset Sheet Questionnaire, which helps us educate you and identify and document your assets and liabilities. Before we dive into the questionnaire, let's go over the definitions of a few important terms you'll need to understand to get the most out of what's to follow."

Key Terms and Concepts[15]

- **Payable on Death (POD) designation**: An arrangement between you and a bank or credit union that designates beneficiaries to receive your assets immediately upon your passing without going through probate.
- **Transfer on Death (TOD) designation**: A way of designating beneficiaries to receive your assets at the time of your death without having to go through probate. This designation also allows you to specify the percentage of assets each person or entity (your "TOD beneficiary") will receive.
- **Per Stirpes designation**: A stipulation that should a beneficiary—usually one of your children—predecease you, the beneficiary's share of the inheritance will go to his or her heirs. Typically, this will be the children from your deceased child, your grandkids.

15 Definitions source: www.Investopedia.com, accessed on December 3, 2015.

- **Per Capita designation**: A stipulation that all living beneficiaries (usually your children) will receive an equal share of the asset in question. If one of the beneficiaries is deceased, then all the shares of the other beneficiaries will be increased accordingly. Typically, this will be the surviving brothers and sisters of that beneficiary.

"These four designations vary from state to state," I said. "Some states don't allow one or the other designation, but they have some other mechanism to take its place. Regardless of where you live, your financial planner should know which ones apply in your particular locale."

"And I assume you know the designations that apply to us here?" Jerry asked.

"Of course. No worries," I replied. "Now, it's also important to note that, when you set up your post-tax accounts and investments, you are not asked for beneficiary designations. You have to take it upon yourself to name the beneficiaries and to title the asset properly with a POD or a TOD, or to title it in the name of a trust. That's what makes setting up post-tax accounts such a tricky proposition, and this is where many people get confused and make mistakes. Thankfully, the same is not true with pre-tax accounts like IRAs, 401(k)s, and 403(b)s. All of these have beneficiary designations built right into the forms you fill out when you set them up.

"This is critical because proper titling and naming of beneficiaries can make the difference between a smooth transfer of assets upon your passing or a tangled mess for your heirs to unravel," I continued. "Worst-case scenario: your estate ends up in probate court. Probate refers to the legal process of determining if a deceased person's will is valid and authentic.

It also refers to the process of administering a deceased person's estate by a court. Probate is something most people want to avoid at all costs. It's expensive, it's time consuming, and it's an invasion of privacy because everything that happens in court is public record. In short, probate can be a very expensive and time-consuming nightmare."

"Tell me about it!" Irene said. "When my Uncle Pete died a few years ago, his estate ended up in probate, and it was a terrible mess for my cousins. It took almost two years to sort out, and it almost caused World War III. We do not want to put our kids through probate."

"We're going to do everything possible to prevent that," I said. "Proper titling and naming of beneficiaries is also essential to ensuring your assets ultimately end up where you want them to. I can't tell you how many times I've seen people accidently disinherit family members or trigger probate because they didn't do a thorough job of titling everything correctly, or they named a primary beneficiary but forgot to designate a secondary or a contingent. By double checking and logging all this information on the Asset Sheet Questionnaire right now, we can mitigate the risk of legal fees and headaches for your family down the road and make sure we set up everything properly so your money goes where you want it to when the time comes."

Jerry and Irene nodded in agreement.

"For that same reason, the Asset Sheet Questionnaire delves into whether each of your accounts has per stirpes or per capita designation," I said. "*Per stirpes* is the Latin term for 'by the branch'; that is, the bloodline. If you list a beneficiary—say, your son, Mike—for a particular asset and he predeceases you, the asset does not automatically transfer to his kids (his bloodline) unless you designated per stirpes for that account. By failing to designate per stirpes, you could unintentionally disinherit your grandchildren. Mike's share would be divided between your remaining children instead."

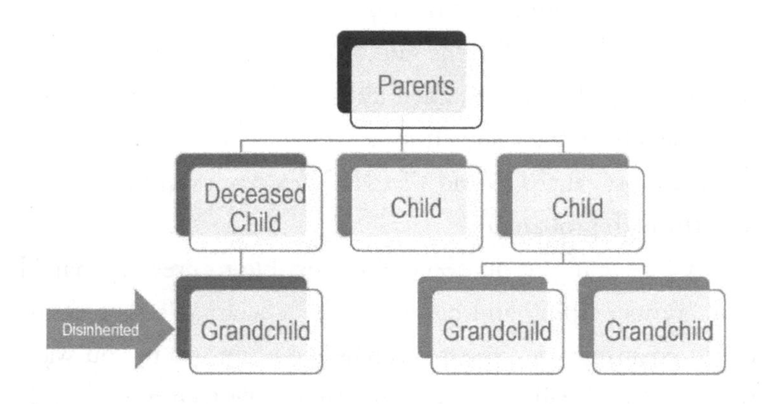

"I'd rather be poked in the eye with a stick than disinherit our grandkids!" Jerry exclaimed.

"Our Asset Sheet Questionnaire will save your eyesight, Jerry," I said with a smile. "Now that you have a handle on the designations and their definitions, understanding the questionnaire will be easy."

CREATING AN ASSET SHEET

I took out a blank Asset Sheet Questionnaire and a pencil, and we began the task of filling it out. The first section of the questionnaire itemized the money Jerry and Irene had in their bank and credit union accounts. This was post-tax money, or money they'd already paid taxes on.

Post-Tax Money

Asset Sheet Questionnaire

Client 1 Name: Irene

Client 2 Name: Jerry   Date: 10-14-14

BANK ACCOUNTS / CREDIT UNIONS (POST-TAX)						
COMPANY NAME	OWNER	TYPE/ DUE DATE	POD / TOD DESIGNATION (Y/N)	PRIMARY / CONTINGENT BENEFICIARY	PER STIRPES / PER CAPITA	VALUE
ABC Credit Union	Joint	Checking	N	None	None	$2,000
Bank 5	Joint	Savings	N	None	None	$13,000
					SUB-TOTAL	$ 15,000

Here, we recorded the names of the bank/credit unions where each account was held, who owned each account (whether it was joint or individual), the type of account(s), if there was a POD/TOD designation in place, who the primary or contingent beneficiaries were (if any), whether there was a per stirpes or per capita designation on each account, and the account's value.

The next section of the questionnaire covered any post-tax investments Jerry and Irene might have had, such as brokerage accounts, annuities, stocks, bonds, and mutual funds. Jerry and Irene didn't know exactly how some of their accounts were set up or titled, so we later conducted a joint call with them and the institutions to verify the account setup and details. They were thankful we helped them gather that information, as they were unsure of the right questions to ask the different companies to get the information we needed to move forward.

Asset Sheet Questionnaire

Client 1 Name: Irene

Client 2 Name: Jerry Date: 10-14-14

BANK ACCOUNTS / CREDIT UNIONS (POST-TAX)

COMPANY NAME	OWNER	TYPE/ DUE DATE	POD / TOD DESIGNATION (Y/N)	PRIMARY / CONTINGENT BENEFICIARY	PER STIRPES / PER CAPITA	VALUE
ABC Credit Union	Joint	Checking	N	None	None	$2,000
Bank 5	Joint	Savings	N	None	None	$13,000
					SUB-TOTAL	$ 15,000

POST-TAX INVESTMENTS

ACCOUNT TYPE* /DUE DATE	COMPANY NAME	OWNER	POD / TOD DESIGNATION (Y/N)	PER STIRPES / PER CAPITA	COST BASIS	VALUE
Brokerage	UBS	Irene/Jerry	N	Per stirpes	$300,000	$350,000
					SUB-TOTAL	$ 350,000
					POST-TAX TOTAL	$ 365,000

** Brokerage Accounts, Annuities, Individual Stocks, Bonds, Mutual Funds, Alternative Investments, etc.*

"Jerry and Irene, notice that the same sort of fact-finding we used to catalog your post-tax bank accounts continues with your post-tax investments," I said. "We want to know who owns each asset; whether beneficiaries are designated—or not, because POD/TOD is one of the only ways to designate beneficiaries on post-tax accounts; if there's per stirpes or per capita designation; and the value. We then add this value to the post-tax assets subtotal from the previous section to arrive at your post-tax total of $365,000."

Pre-Tax Money

PRE-TAX INVESTMENTS								
*TAX STATUS	**ACCOUNT TYPE /DUE DATE	COMPANY NAME	OWNER	PRIMARY / CONTINGENT BENEFICIARY	PER STIRPES / PER CAPITA	COST BASIS	VALUE	
* IRA, 401(k), 403(b), TSP, Pension, Other ** Brokerage Accounts, Annuities, Individual Stocks, Bonds, Mutual Funds, Alternative Investments, etc.								
Pre	403(b)	Community School District	Irene	N	per stirpes	$0	$250,000	
Pre	IRA	UBS	Irene	N	per stirpes	$0	$50,000	
Pre	401(k)	TIAA-CREF	Jerry	N	per stirpes	$0	$150,000	
Pre	IRA	UBS	Jerry	N	per stirpes	$0	$75,000	
			CLIENT 1 Irene		TOTAL	$	300,000	
			CLIENT 2 Jerry		TOTAL	$	225,000	
				TOTAL PRE-TAX INVESTMENTS		$	525,000	

The pre-tax investments section is for the investments that Jerry and Irene had not yet paid taxes on. These included contributions made to an IRA, 401(k), 403(b), or pension that went straight into the investment before any federal, state, or local taxes were taken out. Once we listed all their pre-tax investments on the form, we tallied them up. In the example, notice that we subtotaled Jerry's and Irene's pre-tax investments separately. It was critical for us to know who owned each asset as we designed their customized Bucket Plan.

Now we were ready to log the couples' tax-favored assets, in their case, Irene's Roth IRA.

Tax-Favored Assets

TAX FAVORED ASSETS								
*TAX STATUS	**ACCOUNT TYPE /DUE DATE	COMPANY NAME	OWNER	PRIMARY / CONTINGENT BENEFICIARY	PER STIRPES / PER CAPITA	COST BASIS	PENSION OR DEATH BENEFIT	VALUE
* Roth IRA, Roth 401(k), Roth 403(b), HSA, 529 Plan ** Brokerage Accounts, Annuities, Individual Stocks, Bonds, Mutual Funds, Alternative Investments, etc.								
Post	Roth	UBS	Irene	Jerry	Per stripes	n/a		$50,000
			CLIENT 1 Irene		TOTAL	$		$50,000
			CLIENT 2		TOTAL	$		
				TOTAL TAX FAVORED ASSETS		$		$50,000

"I want to take a moment to emphasize the power of the Roth," I said. "Money deposited into a Roth is post-tax money that grows tax-free and is tax-free at withdrawal if you follow the guidelines the government has put in place. For this reason, it's an important part of most people's retirement planning strategy, including the one we're creating for you. The same is true of life insurance policies.

"Jerry and Irene, life insurance is crucial," I explained, "especially when you consider what we talked about earlier: when one spouse passes away, income goes down and taxes go up for the surviving spouse. Therefore, the life insurance death benefit is a critical part of legacy planning for the survivor because it can serve as a powerful injection of tax-free money that he or she can utilize to offset the lost income and increased tax liability. The surviving spouse can also use it to pay off debt."

At this point, I recalled Jerry and Irene's negative reaction when I brought up the perils of home equity loans during our last meeting, so I decided to ask about it. Jerry revealed that he and Irene had indeed racked up substantial debt—almost

$300,000, to be exact—to put their kids, Mike and Jenny, through college. Mike had recently graduated from law school, and Jenny was in the final stages of earning her doctorate in marine biology. Jerry explained that, to pay for the kids' college, he and Irene had accessed their home equity line of credit, racking up debt upon debt as the tuition payments came due without giving much thought to how they'd pay it back. When Jerry got worried that the interest rates would rise on the home equity line, he and Irene took out a second mortgage on the house to pay off the home equity line so they could lock in a more favorable interest rate. So, although helping their kids achieve their significant educational goals was admirable, it had left the couple upside down on their home.

"We knew it was risky to do that, but it's been worth it," Jerry explained. "Helping Mike and Jen make their dreams come true is the best feeling in the world. Still, I have to admit that it keeps us up at night, Jason. We can't help but worry about what would happen if we couldn't make those payments for some reason."

And that's why we began the process of bumping up Jerry's existing $50,000 life insurance to a $300,000 death benefit right then and there, with the idea that the death benefit would be earmarked for paying off the mortgage, if necessary. We wanted to be certain that, if something happened to him before that college debt was repaid, Irene would get to keep their home. Irene had unfortunately suffered some recent medical issues that made her ineligible to increase her death benefit, but Jerry felt confident that, if she were to pass away first, he could continue with the consulting work he currently was doing and continue to make the payments.

LIFE INSURANCE						
COMPANY NAME	PREMIUM	INSURED/ OWNER/ POLICY TYPE	PRIMARY / CONTINGENT BENEFICIARY	PER STIRPES / PER CAPITA	DEATH BENEFIT	CASH VALUE
Met Life	72 mo	Jerry	Irene (p)	Per Capita	300,000	
NYL	1200yr	Irene	Jerry (p)	Per Capita	100,000	25,000
				TOTAL DEATH BENEFIT	$	400,000
				TOTAL CASH VALUE	$	25,000

We were also particularly interested in the cash value Irene had built up in her policy because we knew we could utilize it as a resource for tax-free withdrawals later, if need be. The cash value of a life insurance policy is the amount that has been paid in over the course of the contract through premiums, as well as any interest growth. It is the amount that the contract would pay out to the owner if it were cancelled or surrendered, but it also may be available to access during life via loans while keeping the contract intact. (Note: term life insurance does not accumulate cash value, which is part of why the premiums are much lower compared to whole or universal life insurance.) As I explained to Jerry and Irene, cash value life insurance is very similar to a Roth IRA because, like Roth, the money goes in as post-tax money, grows tax-free, and comes out tax-free (if you follow the government's rules, of course). It basically works like a Roth where the money is held inside a life insurance policy.

OK	GOOD	BEST ✓
Pre-tax money	Post-tax money	**Roth and Cash Value in Life Insurance**

"Like your other investments, your life insurance policy is an asset class that must be properly managed if it's to realize its full potential," I said. "In many cases, we will be able to make positive changes to your current life insurance portfolio. We may be able to decrease your premiums, convert it to a paid-up policy, increase the death benefit for the same amount of premium you're currently paying, or sell it for you to a third party that will pay you more than you would get if you cashed it in."

"Wow, I had no idea we had those kinds of options," said Jerry.

"There are a lot of great things that can be done with old life insurance policies, Jerry, and it's important that we review all your options as part of your overall retirement plan."

We went back to the Asset Sheet Questionnaire. We were starting to get a detailed map of Jerry and Irene's entire financial landscape now . . .

Real Estate/Business Interests

TYPE	OWNER	PER STIRPES / PER CAPITA	COST BASIS	POD / TOD DESIGNATION	VALUE
Primary Home	JTWROS	N/a	95,000	N	320,000
Lake Cabin	JTWROS	N/a	100,000	N	125,000
			TOTAL REAL ESTATE	$	445,000

Jerry and Irene had no business interests, but clearly it was important to note their real estate holdings, who owned them, whether there was a POD/TOD designation, the per stirpes/ per capita status, and the value of the real estate. We included cost basis because it's important when planning tax ramifications for heirs. Cost basis is what you paid for the home plus any updates or additions you've done to the property.

"Although it's not the case for you two, we've seen many instances in which a house or other property is held in only one spouse's name," I explained. "When that spouse passes away, it can trigger a costly and time-consuming probate process for the survivor. That's why it was critical for us to review the ownership and titling of all your real estate assets. We have a little work to do on your real estate designations, but once we're through, you'll be in fine shape."

"That's good to know," Jerry said. "Now I understand what you meant when you said The Bucket Plan process gives you peace of mind."

"Next up: debt," I said.

Debt

DEBT					
DEBT HOLDER NAME	OWNER	TYPE	RELATED ASSET	INTEREST RATE	DEBT AMOUNT
Fifth Third	Joint	Mortgage	Primary Home	5.25%	298,000
Fifth Third	Joint	Mortgage	Lake Cabin	4.875%	24,000
				TOTAL DEBT	($ 322,000)

Here we listed the debt Jerry and Irene had, who owned it, the type of debt and its corresponding asset, the interest rate, and how much was still owed.

"Again, this list is not only important for legacy planning

for your surviving spouse and for settling your estate in the future," I explained, "but also so we can get strategic about the way we handle that debt right now. Let's use credit card debt as an example. Imagine that you had a credit card in both your names. You usually pay off that bill every month, but let's say you spent down most of your money and maxed out your credit card on medical expenses because Jerry had a catastrophic health event—"

"Stop. I don't even want to *think* about that, let alone *talk* about it," Irene said.

"We have to talk about it, Irene," Jerry replied. "We need to know that we've got all the bases covered. Go ahead, Jason."

"So, you have a credit card with a high balance, and Jerry passes," I continued. "Since the card was in both of your names, Irene, you'd be solely responsible for that debt after Jerry's passing. But had that card been only in the primary breadwinner's name, which is Jerry, the credit card company would simply write off the debt after his death. Irene, the surviving spouse, could walk away without owing anything."

"I had no idea," Jerry said.

"It's true. I've actually seen it happen. Last year, a woman came to see us for help. Her husband had gone into the nursing home, and they'd spent down all their assets on his care. They were essentially wiped out because she'd run up a bunch of credit card debt hiring nurses and physical therapists and paying for his prescription drugs. And then he died. Because the credit card was in his name, they were able to write off that debt. It was a huge game-changer for her. She was amazed that she could walk away from it. Another example would be leasing a car. When you go to lease a car, the dealership will usually try to get you and your spouse to put the lease in both of your names. Have you ever wondered why they are so adamant about trying to do that?"

Jerry and Irene shook their heads.

"It's because the same principle applies; if both names are on the lease and one spouse passes away, the survivor will still be liable for the debt. Suddenly, you're a widow or widower who's responsible for paying for two cars! But if you put the lease in the primary breadwinner's name and he or she passes away, the survivor simply turns in the keys and walks away. It doesn't matter if you have three days or three years left on that lease."

"Wow," Jerry said. "I'm going to let my brothers and sister know about this. This is really important information to have."

"Yes, it is because, remember: when a spouse passes away, income goes down and taxes go up for the survivor," I said. "Any relief we can give that surviving spouse can have a huge impact. That's why it's critical to know about options like this as a last resort. But, if your brothers and sister reside in a community property state like Arizona, California, Idaho, Louisiana, Nevada, New Mexico, Texas, Washington, or Wisconsin, this wouldn't work the same way for them, so they'd need to speak to an advisor if this is a concern. The bottom line is that we want to examine, understand, and get strategic about managing your debt. This section of the Asset Sheet Questionnaire helps us do that."

And last but certainly not least, we brought to light something Jerry and Irene would be forced to deal with eventually—the taxes on their pre-tax money.

Liabilities

CURRENT ESTIMATED TAX LIABILITIES (Taxes: IRA/401k Liquidation, ROTH Conversion, Estate Taxes)			
TYPE OF LIABILITY	OWNER	RELATED ASSET	AMOUNT
IRA Income Tax Liability when withdrawn	Jerry/Irene Beneficiaries	IRA	210,000
		TOTAL LIABILITIES	($ 210,000)

This is where we listed the estimated tax liability Jerry and Irene (or their family) would have to pay at some point when they started to draw down or liquidate their IRA, 401(k), or any other pre-tax money. In some cases, people will start to pay a little bit of tax annually by converting some of their IRA money each year to a Roth; by doing this, they'll start to whittle away at their tax liability slowly over time versus leaving their spouse or kids to deal with it later. In Jerry and Irene's case, we estimated that Jerry, Irene, or their family would have to pony up somewhere around $210,000 of income tax liability based on the current value of their pre-tax IRA money.

"Jerry and Irene, whether you realize it or not, you're in a partnership with the federal government when it comes to your pre-tax money," I explained. "Uncle Sam owns a big chunk of it—your estimated tax liability—and that money has to be paid at some point. There are many ways of buying your way out of this partnership with the federal government. You can pay the tax liability during your lifetime, or you can have your spouse or family pay it after your passing."

"Sheesh. I think we ought to be able to list Uncle Sam as a dependent on our next tax return," Jerry joked. "Is that doable?"

"Sorry, Jerry," I said with a laugh, "that's not an option. You simply must pay that tax liability. *When* you pay is your choice, though. Do you want to proactively defuse that tax time bomb, or do you want to kick the can down the road and follow the government's plan? Part of the government's plan is to force you to take the money out via required minimum distributions, or RMDs, at age seventy and a half. The other part of the government's plan is that, when you pass away, your spouse or kids may end up paying it in full and potentially from a much higher tax bracket. There are things we can do right now to lower your tax liability and put more of a strategy in place versus blindly following the government's plan.

"And that's why estimated tax liability is listed on the Asset Sheet Questionnaire. Tax liability isn't exactly debt, but it's still money we owe . . . and, as the estimated tax liability section example shows, it can be substantial. There are some interesting ways to offset that, but we can't even begin to address this liability until we know it's there and can calculate the potential extent of it.

"That's what makes the Asset Sheet Questionnaire such a phenomenal tool in The Bucket Plan planning process," I said to Jerry and Irene. "It shines a bright light on shadowy things like future tax liability, which allows us to get strategic and intervene before it's too late."

THE RESULT: EVERYTHING IN ITS PLACE

Once we'd finished filling out Jerry and Irene's Asset Sheet Questionnaire, we extrapolated all the data and created their final customized Asset Sheet.

"The Asset Sheet is an extremely important document," I explained. "If you've ever owned a business, you likely had what's called a balance sheet: one consolidated document listing all your company's assets and liabilities. Well, our Asset Sheet is sort of like your own personal balance sheet. It records every asset in your estate, with the exception of personal items. It also lists all your liabilities and debt. We then take the value of those assets and subtract the debt to arrive at your net worth."

Here's Jerry and Irene's final Asset Sheet:

	OWNER	TYPE / DUE DATE	PENSION or DEATH BENEFIT	MARKET VALUE	CATEGORY TOTAL
BANK ACCOUNTS					
ABC Credit Union	Joint	Checking		$ 2,000	
Bank 5	Joint	Savings		$ 13,000	
SUB-TOTAL					$ 15,000
POST-TAX INVESTMENTS					
UBS	Joint	Brokerage		$ 350,000	
SUB-TOTAL					$ 350,000
PRE-TAX INVESTMENTS					
Community School District	Irene	403(b)		$ 250,000	
UBS	Irene	IRA		$ 50,000	
TIAA-CREF	Jerry	401(k)		$ 150,000	
UBS	Jerry	IRA		$ 75,000	
SUB-TOTAL					$ 525,000
ROTH IRA / 401k ETC.					
UBS	Irene	Post-Tax Roth		$ 50,000	
SUB-TOTAL					$ 50,000
LIFE INSURANCE					
Met Life	Jerry		$ 300,000		
NYL	Irene		$ 100,000	$ 25,000	
SUB-TOTAL					$ 25,000
REAL ESTATE					
Primary Home	JTWROS			$ 320,000	
Lake Cabin	JTWROS			$ 125,000	
SUB-TOTAL					$ 445,000
DEBT					
Fifth Third	Joint	Mortgage		$ (24,000)	
Fifth Third	Joint	Mortgage		$ (298,000)	
SUB-TOTAL					$ (322,000)
ESTIMATED NET WORTH					**$ 1,088,000**
ESTIMATED TAX LIABILITIES					
IRA Income Tax Liability when withdrawn	Jerry/ Irene	IRA		$ (210,000)	
Numbers are estimated and approximate					

"Since we'll update your Asset Sheet every year during your annual review, it is a living document," I explained to Jerry and Irene. "The Asset Sheet will make it easy for you to track how all your investments are doing year after year and to check your account balances at a glance. Recall the lesson on sequence of returns risk: *it's not about average rate of return; it's about account balances.* With the Asset Sheet, you'll be able to keep an eye on those all-important account balances with ease."

"That's so much better than the system I have now," Jerry said. "I spend way too much time and energy trying to keep track of our balances."

"The Asset Sheet will solve that problem for you," I said. "Another advantage of having an Asset Sheet is that, when you pass away, your children won't have to take off work for weeks digging through safety deposit boxes, drawers, file cabinets, mail, and everything else you own trying to figure out what you have to settle your affairs. Since the document provides an inventory of everything you have, your kids will possess a one-page snapshot that outlines your entire financial situation. And because we fixed all the asset titling and beneficiaries, they should be able to avoid the dreaded entanglement of probate court.

"The Asset Sheet is also a way to monitor cash flow," I continued. "Not only does it catalog your assets in one place, but it also helps us keep track of when your CDs mature, when your 401(k)s and other pre-tax accounts become eligible for rollovers, and so on. It's also a great way for us to monitor your spending habits. If we notice that you're accumulating a lot of money in checking and savings, we can examine positioning that money in a more strategic way rather than just letting it languish in the bank. Conversely, if we see that more money than we anticipated is being depleted from your checking and savings, we can take steps to ensure that your spending doesn't get out of line, or we can increase withdrawals from your Soon bucket.

"The Asset Sheet also helps us compartmentalize your money based on tax qualifications and tax treatment of those monies," I said. "To create a sound financial plan for your retirement, it's critical for us to distinguish your post-tax and pre-tax money. Now, I'm going to let you in on a little secret. Many of us financial planners call pre-tax money 'bad money' and post-tax money 'good money.'"

"Where I come from, all money is good money," Jerry said.

"Oh, don't get me wrong, it *is* all good," I said. "But from our perspective as planners, pre-tax money is bad because the government owns a big percentage of it. You're required to follow a ton of rules with pre-tax money, but post-tax money is yours, free and clear. There are no rules. You can hold a post-tax investment until you pass away, and then your family can sell it and pay no taxes in most cases because of capital gains taxes being waived at the time of the inheritance due to automatic step up in cost basis. You can own it jointly, you can own it individually, and you can withdraw it whenever you want."

"Or you can put it under your mattress, or bury it in the backyard," Jerry said.

"Probably not the best idea, but you can," I laughed. "You can't do that with pre-tax money because you'd have to pay all that tax in one lump sum when you moved it out of the IRA or 401(k) it was in, if you didn't put it back into that same pre-tax status.

"The point is that we want to categorize and thoroughly understand all your assets so we can funnel your bad pre-tax money into good post-tax money—or, better yet, into a Roth through contributions or conversions, or into a cash value life insurance policy, if you qualify, which also offers you better tax options and more freedom. The Asset Sheet lays everything out for us and for you. It's like a game, and we're keeping track of the score."

"Our odds for winning this game are looking better with each passing minute," Irene said. "I can't wait to see what's coming next!"

RECAP

Here are the important things the Asset Sheet Questionnaire does for you:

- It gives you and us a thorough understanding of your financial situation.
- It leads to the creation of your customized Asset Sheet, which gives you a one-stop location for tracking your account balances and cash flow from year to year.
- It helps your advisor compartmentalize your assets so he or she can work to turn more of your "bad" pre-tax money into "good" post-tax money.
- It provides you and your advisor with debt identification and sets the stage for elimination.
- It estimates your tax liabilities so your advisor can devise a proactive strategy for defusing that ticking tax time bomb rather than letting it blow up on you and your family later.
- It captures your beneficiary information and ensures proper asset titling so you can (1) avoid putting your family through probate upon your passing and (2) avoid unintentionally disinheriting your loved ones.
- It makes settling your estate much easier for your heirs because they will be able to see all your assets, debts, and liabilities in one simple document.

Chapter 5

THE INCOME GAP ASSESSMENT

Determining If There Will Be a Retirement Income Deficit (or Excess) and If So, How Much

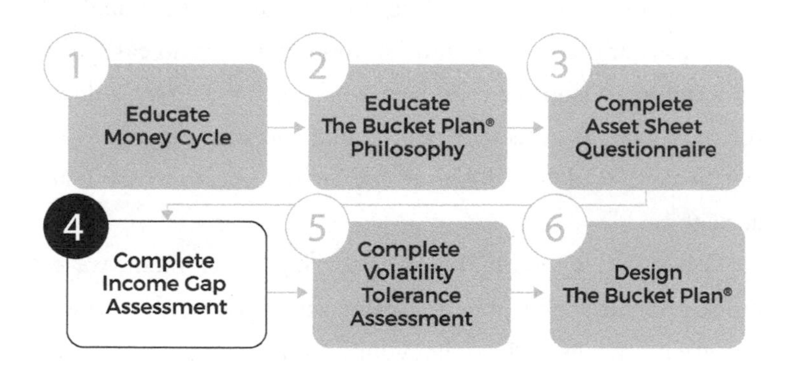

Once we had a thorough understanding of Jerry and Irene's assets, debts, and tax liabilities, we turned to the next segment of The Bucket Plan® planning process: the Income Gap Assessment.

"Jerry and Irene, to create your Bucket Plan, we need to understand how much money you will need for day-to-day living in retirement and determine where that money will come from," I said. "There are two ways we can gain that understanding. The first is to work up a full-blown budget. Some folks require a comprehensive budget because they have a complex financial situation, or they want one because they enjoy the detail-oriented budgeting process."

"I don't think we fit either of those descriptions," Jerry said.

"Me neither," said Irene. "What's the alternative?"

"The second option—the Income Gap Assessment—is the way to go for most people, including you two," I replied. "The Income Gap Assessment is a simple, one-page tool for discovering if there is now, or if there is going to be, a gap between your expected net income in retirement and the amount you'll need for living expenses. Filling out this document enables us to get to your income gap number more quickly and easily than undertaking a complete budget workup. It's a great solution for most people, especially people like you who are still working, because we have a baseline for the income to which you're accustomed."

I continued, "With the Income Gap Assessment, we can quickly identify how much income you're currently receiving net-after-taxes, as well as what your fixed retirement income will be so we can expose any gaps that will need to be filled by pulling from your liquid investable assets. Without such an assessment, it's difficult to know how much income you'll need each month. Not knowing your gap number prevents you from strategically investing and saving based on a specific need or goal."

"It sounds like this assessment will take some of the

guesswork out of our retirement planning," Jerry said. "I like that. Let's do it." At that, we set to work filling out Jerry and Irene's Income Gap Assessment:

Client(s) Name: Jerry & Irene   Date: 10-14-14

Client Name	Source	Amount	Multiplied by (to total one year)	Annual Total
Current Amount Deposited Into Checking (Net Income After Taxes)				
Irene	Community School Dist.	1583	12	19,000
Jerry	Del Greco Construction	1462	26	38,000
			Annual Income Loss	($ 57,000)
Fixed Income in Retirement (Pensions/SS)				
Irene	Social Security	1083	12	13,000
Jerry	Social Security	583	12	7,000
			Fixed Income Addition	$ 20,000
Adjustments				
Increased Expenses in Retirement (income tax, health insurance, travel, etc.)				
				($)
				($)
				($)
Decreased Expenses in Retirement (savings, mortgage paid off, health insurance, etc.)				
Joint	Lake Cabin	1000	12	$ 12,000
				$
				$
			Adjustments Subtotal	$ 12,000
			(Annual Income) + Fixed Income +/- Adjustments = Annual Income Gap Total*	($ 25,000)

ASK: *How much of this income gap would you want guaranteed in your financial plan?*

*Tax pro forma must be completed in order to determine tax liability

In the first section of the assessment, we logged the amount deposited into Jerry and Irene's checking account each month. This was their net income after taxes. In this scenario, Irene was semi-retired from teaching. She'd taught school full-time for fourteen years, but she'd left the workforce to stay home with the kids when they were young. Now, she was working a couple of days a week tutoring children at the Community School District, where she was earning $1,583 a month (or about $19,000 annually). Jerry was semi-retired from his construction management career. He was working part-time as a consultant for his friend, the owner of Del Greco's Construction, where he was bringing home $1,462 every two weeks (or around $38,000 annually). Remember, we were recording net-after-taxes income. We then added Jerry and Irene's annual incomes together to arrive at an annual income subtotal of $57,000. This was the amount they were living on at the time of this assessment and the amount that would be going away when they retired fully.

Once we knew how much Jerry and Irene were depositing into their checking account, I asked them which of these three scenarios best described their financial status at the end of most months:

- They had money left over to save.
- They broke even.
- They ran up debt.

"We usually break even," Jerry replied. "Well, unless there's a big sale at Macy's . . . am I right, Irene?"

"Or the Indians are on a hot streak and you *must* buy tickets to every game of the home stand," Irene retorted. "Or it's time for your annual fly-fishing trip with your buddies. Or the Rolling Stones are coming to town. Or it's Girl Scout cookie season. Or—"

"Okay, okay. I think he gets the picture," Jerry laughed. "In all seriousness Jason, we almost always break even or have a little cash left over at the end of the month."

"That's what I figured," I said. "Most people break even

or save money every month. If you're going into debt most months, then we'd need to have a whole other conversation."

We moved on to the next section of the assessment: Fixed Income at Retirement. How much money would Jerry and Irene be receiving from their pension(s) and/or Social Security each month? As indicated on the form, neither would be receiving pension benefits. Both would be taking Social Security at age sixty-two, which totaled to about $20,000 a year. We ran a Social Security report to demonstrate the option of waiting to full retirement age or delaying until age seventy to maximize their benefits. Applying early versus waiting until full retirement age meant a 25 percent reduction in benefits, along with missing the additional (approximate) eight percent annual growth incentive they could realize by waiting until age seventy. Even with these considerations in mind, Jerry and Irene ultimately decided to take their benefits as soon as they were available.

As Jerry explained it, "My dad spent his whole life complaining about having to pay into Social Security, and then he died of a heart attack the year before he retired. He never got to collect a penny. So, I want to start drawing my benefits as soon as I'm eligible."

"Fair enough," I replied.

The next section of the assessment is for cataloging any increased expenses that might be coming up in retirement. This could be tax increases, health insurance premiums that your employer paid, increased travel, and the like. None of that applied to Jerry and Irene.

Next, we logged any major expenses that would be ending

for them during retirement because it's just as important to factor in these anticipated drops in expenses as it is to note any increases. In Jerry and Irene's example, they were on track to pay off the mortgage on their lake cabin in less than two years, giving them a reduction in their living expenses of $1,000 each month. Multiply that by twelve months: $12,000.

We took the combined $57,000 annual net income that Jerry and Irene were currently living on and would need in retirement. We then considered the $20,000 Social Security they would receive annually in retirement, as well as the $12,000 annual mortgage expense that was going away, and we came up with Jerry and Irene's income gap number: $25,000. This was the difference between how much money they would receive from their fixed income at retirement and how much they would need for living expenses. This was approximately how much they were going to have to draw annually from liquid investable assets in retirement.

Once we had all this information, we entered the numbers into our tax software to see if we needed to draw a little more to cover income tax liability to deliver the after-tax income they need. We always do this as a best practice, just to make sure we're recommending withdrawals sufficient to cover this occasionally substantial expense. Even after factoring in drawing the $25K from their pre-tax, Jerry and Irene's tax liability would be less than $40 a month, so they didn't think it was necessary to factor in additional withdrawals for tax liability.

"This assessment has completely taken the mystery out of calculating our retirement income needs," Irene said. "Before today, all we could do was guess. Now we *know*. Such a relief!"

More Than Just Identifying Gaps

I told Jerry and Irene that sometimes, when we take people through the Income Gap Assessment exercise, we come to the realization that they will not have an income *deficit* entering retirement but an *overabundance*, an excess cash flow. Usually these are people who were lucky enough to get large pension benefits from where they worked.

I explained it to the couple this way: "If there will be excess cash flow in your retirement—or, if you're a pre-retiree and there is currently an excess—we want to know because this presents the opportunity for us to do even more strategic tax planning, focusing on reducing tax liability for the future by paying some of those future tax liabilities now while taxes are still near historic lows. It also changes how we frame up your Bucket Plan. If you won't need to draw from your liquid investable assets to fill an income gap right away, then the Soon bucket becomes money you *may* need soon, and not money you will *definitely* need to create a stable income stream.

"We also need to consider the required minimum distributions (RMDs) that start happening at age seventy and a half," I continued, "because you will be forced to draw from your money then, whether you want to or not. In some excess cash-flow scenarios, setting aside multiple years of that forced income (RMDs) will be your only Soon bucket money. In that case, it will be crucial to protect and preserve it and not subject it to sequence of returns risk, as I explained to you in our first meeting."

Now that we had total clarity on the cash-flow situation Jerry and Irene would be facing in retirement, we moved on to assessing their tolerance for investment risk or volatility.

RECAP

Here are the important things to remember about the Income Gap Assessment:

- The Income Gap Assessment is a simple, one-page tool that helps you and your advisor calculate how much money you will need for day-to-day living in retirement and identify where that money will come from. It's much simpler than creating a full-blown budget.
- Your advisor can use this tool to determine if there will be a gap between your expected net income in retirement and the amount you'll need for living expenses.
- When completing the Income Gap Assessment, you are forced to think through and plan for the potential increased and decreased expenses in retirement.
- It also identifies if there will be an excess cash flow in retirement, making it possible to get even more strategic with your tax planning and investing.

Chapter 6

THE VOLATILITY TOLERANCE ANALYSIS

Assessing Attitudes About Risk and Volatility in the Soon and Later Time Frames

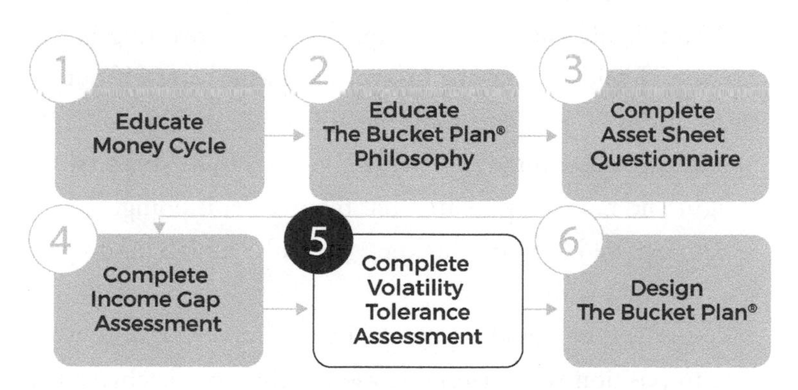

After finishing the Income Gap Assessment, we always make a point of talking with our clients about the *three principles of sound investing* because these principles are key to understanding the next segment of The Bucket Plan® planning process.

"The first principle of sound investing is *time horizon*," I explained to Jerry and Irene. "It takes time to grow money.

Establishing Now and Soon buckets as part of your customized Bucket Plan buys you time to focus on the growth of the money in your Later bucket so you can have financial security in your retirement while leaving a legacy for each other and your loved ones.

"The second principle of sound investing is *diversification*," I continued. "You don't want to keep all your eggs in one basket because if something bad happens to that basket—"

"No omelets for you," Jerry said.

"That's right, Jerry. Sound investing requires that you spread your assets among the various types of investment vehicles and markets so that, when one segment takes a nosedive, it doesn't have a negative impact or as much of an impact on the money you've allocated elsewhere.

"And finally, the third principle of sound investing is *risk tolerance*," I said. "You want to avoid stressing yourself out by taking on more risk and more volatility in your investments than your peace of mind can stand. You need to be able to sleep at night and not worry about what the market is doing."

Irene patted Jerry on the knee. "I think he's talking to you, dear," she said with a wink.

"On the other hand, if you can handle more volatility, we'll want to position your investable assets properly to achieve the growth you desire," I said. "And that's why we have you undergo a Volatility Tolerance Analysis now, so we can measure your tolerance for risk and market volatility and then allocate your assets accordingly. We want to be sure the customized Bucket Plan we create for you stays within your investment comfort zone while simultaneously working to reach your goals and expectations for growth."

A Distinctive Kind of Risk Assessment

"Jason, something just occurred to me," Irene said. "My friend Denise told me her financial advisor gave her a questionnaire that sounds very similar to what you're talking about. She called it a 'risk assessment.' Is that the same thing as your Volatility Tolerance Analysis?"

"That's a great question," I replied. "Most advisors do use a standard risk assessment that's based on a combination of psychology and statistics to evaluate their clients' risk tolerance, but our Volatility Tolerance Analysis is different. We dig deeper by dividing our questionnaire into two parts so we can assess how much volatility you're comfortable taking on with both the money you may need to access soon and the money that has the benefit of a longer investment time horizon. We need to understand how open or averse to risk you are in *both* scenarios because you'll invest short-term money—that's your Soon bucket—quite a bit differently than long-term money, which will be in your Later bucket.

"This tool is an important part of the educational process we take all our clients through," I continued. "Not only does it help us get a feel for your attitudes about risk, but it's also an eye-opener for you. Many people are surprised by how much or how little volatility they are prepared to accept, and how their tolerance changes depending on whether the money in question is a long-term or potentially short-term investment. Let's jump right in and assess your attitude about your Later bucket money, the money with the benefit of a long investment time horizon. You won't draw from this bucket for at least ten years."

Jerry, Irene, and I filled out the first portion of the assessment, and I tallied their score to identify where they landed on the chart.

Later Bucket Volatility Tolerance

The first 7 questions of this assessment are related to your Later Bucket of money.

Based on our Bucket Plan Approach, this is the money which you do not intend to access for ten years or more. The following 7 questions will give your advisor a better understanding of how much volatility you are comfortable taking on with your Later Bucket money, which has a longer time horizon to be put to work.

1. When do you expect to start drawing income from the later bucket?

- ○ Not for at least 30+ years (5pts.)
- ○ In 25-30 years (4pts.)
- ○ In 20-25 years (3pts.)
- ● In 15-20 years (2pts.)
- ○ In 10-15 years (1pt.)

Score: 2

2. Assuming normal market conditions, what would you expect from your later bucket investments over time.

- ○ To outpace the stock market (5pts.)
- ● To generally keep pace with the stock market (4pts.)
- ○ To trail the stock market, but make modest profit (3pts.)
- ○ To have a high degree of stability, but make small profits (2pts.)
- ○ To be little affected by what happens in the stock market (1pt.)

Score: 4

3. I am comfortable with investments that may go down in value from time to time, if they offer the potential for higher returns.

- ● Agree Strongly (5pts.)
- ○ Agree (4pts.)
- ○ Agree Somewhat (3pts.)
- ○ Disagree (2pts.)
- ○ Disagree Strongly (1pt.)

Score: 5

4. Suppose the stock market performs unusually poorly over the next decade. What would you expect from the investments in your later bucket?

- ○ To lose money (5pts.)
- ● To make nothing (4pts.)
- ○ To make a little gain (3pts.)
- ○ To make a modest gain (2pts.)
- ○ To be little affected by what happens in the stock market (1pt.)

Score: 4

5. **Which of these plans would you choose for your investment dollars?**

- ○ You invest your dollars in fixed guaranteed investments. (1pt.)
- ○ You go for maximum diversity by dividing your dollars among many different investments to achieve a moderate rate of return with a moderate level of risk. (3pts.)
- ● You would put your dollars into one investment category or class with the highest rate of return and the most risk. (5pts.)

Score: 5

6. **Considering your later bucket, which of these statements would best describe your attitudes about next year's performance of your investments?**

- ○ Who cares? One year means nothing. (5pts.)
- ● I wouldn't worry about losses in that time frame. (4pts.)
- ○ If I suffered a loss greater than 10%, I'd get concerned. (3pts.)
- ○ I can only tolerate small short-term losses. (2pts.)
- ○ I'd have a hard time stomaching any losses. (1pt.)

Score: 4

7. **You have an opportunity to fund an underwater salvage operation to recover sunken treasure. The chances of finding the vessel are 25%. But, if recovered, you could earn 75-100 times your investment. How much do you invest?**

- ○ One year's salary (5pts.)
- ● Six months' salary (4pts.)
- ○ Three months' salary (3pts.)
- ○ One month's salary (2pts.)
- ○ Nothing at all (1pt.)

Score: 4

Later Bucket Total Score: 28

Later Bucket Category: Growth

Later Bucket Volatility Tolerance Scoring	
Volatility Tolerance Category	Score
Capital Preservation	7-10
Stable	11-14
Conservative	15-18
Balanced	19-22
Moderate	23-26
Growth	27-30
Aggressive	31-35

"Jerry and Irene, with a score of 28, you fall into the Growth category when it comes to investing in your Later bucket," I explained. "That means you have a higher tolerance for market volatility than people whose score puts them in the Capital Preservation, Stable, Conservative, Balanced, or Moderate categories, yet not as much tolerance as people whose score landed them in the Aggressive category. Consequently, you would probably be most comfortable with a growth-oriented portfolio designed to achieve market-like returns with a primary objective of capital appreciation."

Jerry and Irene said they agreed with that outcome. Next, I had them answer five simple but revealing questions about their volatility tolerance related to their Soon bucket money—the money they would need sooner rather than later for income or withdrawals during retirement.

Soon Bucket Volatility Tolerance

The next five questions relate to money you may need to access sooner rather than later.

1. When do you expect to take your first distribution from your investments in your soon bucket?

- ○ Currently taking distributions or will in the next 1-2 years (1pt.)
- ● 3 to 5 years (2pts.)
- ○ 6 to 9 years (3pts.)
- ○ 10 or more years (4pts.)

Score: 2

2. While asking yourself, "What do I most want to accomplish?" select the objective that best fits the purpose of your soon bucket.

- ● My investment should be safe. Preserving value is my focus, and I do not want to risk losing my principal. (1pt.)
- ○ My investment should generate regular income I can spend. (2pts.)
- ○ My investment should generate some current income and grow in value over time. (3pts.)
- ○ My investment should achieve capital appreciation over time with nominal income. (4pts.)
- ○ My investment should achieve maximum capital appreciation. There is no need for current income. (5pts.)

Score: 1

3. How would you rate your willingness to take on market volatility with accounts you may depend on for potential distributions sooner rather than later?

- ○ No volatility (1pt.)
- ○ Low volatility (2pts.)
- ● Average volatility (3pts.)
- ○ Above Average volatility (4pts.)

Score: 3

4. In your soon bucket, for money that you may need to withdraw sooner rather than later, how much could your account balance go down in a single year before you feel uncomfortable?

- ○ Any fall would make me feel uncomfortable (1pt.)
- ○ 5% (2pts.)
- ● 10% (3pts.)
- ○ 15% (4pts.)
- ○ 20% (5pts.)
- ○ 25% (6pts.)

Score: 3

I tallied their responses for this portion of the questionnaire and identified where they landed on the corresponding score chart.

5. Most portfolios have a mix of investments. Some of the investments may have higher expected returns but with higher volatility, while some may have lower volatility with lower expected returns. *(For example, equity mutual funds correspond to high volatility, and fixed vehicles such as bonds correspond to lower volatility.)*

In your soon bucket, which mix of investments do you find most appealing for accounts you may depend on for distributions sooner rather later? *(Please select one sample portfolio.)*

Choose One	Sample Portfolio	High Volatility / Return	Low Volatility / Return	
○	Portfolio 1	0%	100%	(1pt.)
◉	Portfolio 2	20%	80%	(2pts.)
○	Portfolio 3	40%	60%	(3pts.)
○	Portfolio 4	60%	40%	(4pts.)
○	Portfolio 5	80%	20%	(5pts.)

Score: 2

Soon Bucket Total Score: 11

Soon Bucket Category: Stable

Soon Bucket Volatility Tolerance Scoring	
Volatility Tolerance Category	**Score**
Capital Preservation	5-8
Stable	9-12
Conservative	13-16
Balanced	17-20
Moderate Growth	20-24

"In this section, you scored 11, putting you in the Stable category," I said. "The primary objective for investors in this category is capital preservation, yet they're willing to accept a small exposure to equities to increase their potential returns."

Soon Bucket Volatility Tolerance

Score: 11 Category: Stable

Later Bucket Volatility Tolerance

Score: 28 Category: Growth

Capital Preservation
Capital preservation is focused on achieving maximum income with preservation of capital as its primary objective. The typical investor that fits into this category is very risk averse and not willing to take on any amount of principal volatility.

Stable
Stable is focused on achieving current income with a primary objective of preservation, but willing to accept a small exposure to equities to help increase potential returns. The typical investor that fits into this category is willing to take on a small amount of principal volatility.

Conservative
Conservative is focused on achieving conservative growth utilizing a conservatively weighted mix of investments. The typical investor that fits into this category is comfortable with a below-average amount of principal volatility.

Balanced
Balanced is focused on achieving equal balance between preservation and growth. The typical investor that fits into this category is comfortable with an average amount of principal volatility.

Moderate
Moderate is focused on achieving moderate growth utilizing a growth weighted mix of investments. The typical investor that fits into this category is comfortable with an above-average amount of principal volatility.

Growth
Growth is focused on achieving market-like returns with a primary objective of capital appreciation. The typical investor that fits into this category is willing to take on a large amount of principal volatility.

Aggressive
Aggressive is focused on achieving long-term maximum growth as its primary objective utilizing a portfolio of equity investments. The typical investor that fits into this category is comfortable with a very high amount of principal volatility.

"Now, younger or more aggressive investors might decide to take on more risk in their Soon bucket than you're going to be taking," I continued. "On the other hand, those who will be drawing heavily from their Soon bucket in retirement may decide they don't want *any* stocks/equities in their Soon bucket—"

"That's the way I feel," Jerry said. "Even though we scored in the Stable category, I'm not comfortable with stocks or equities in our Soon bucket. What do you think, Irene?"

"I agree. Our peace of mind is the top priority."

"Understood," I said. "In that case, let's check the 'no' box where it asks if you agree with the results of the Volatility Tolerance Analysis, and then let's talk about your options."

Do you agree with the results of this Volatility Tolerance Analysis?

☐ Yes

☑ No

If you do not agree with the tolerance category that your results suggest, please detail which category you believe would be more appropriate and WHY (Client and Advisor may provide perspective).

We don't want any equities in our Soon Bucket

"Jerry and Irene, as you can see, the Volatility Tolerance Analysis took the mystery out of positioning your assets for a worry-free retirement," I said. "Retirees who don't undertake such an analysis face the danger of three bad outcomes. First, they may assume too much risk with their Soon bucket and suffer losses from which they can't recover."

"Like my brother Ted," Jerry said.

"Unfortunately, yes," I replied. "Second, they may not invest properly for long-term growth with their Later bucket, which leads to underperformance. And third, they can't sleep at night because they've taken on more risk than they can stomach. A big part of our jobs as holistic financial planners is to ensure you feel comfortable with your portfolio and comprehensive plan."

"It's kind of amazing," Irene said. "Answering the questions on the Volatility Tolerance Analysis took less than ten minutes, but it was ten minutes well spent because it gave us a really good idea of our preferences and feelings about volatility related to our money."

Jerry chimed in, "Not only that, but it also helped us come up with a feeling for the investment strategies in each bucket that make the most sense for our comfort level. I know I sound like a broken record, but it's all about being able to sleep at night. I had no idea it could be so simple."

RECAP

Here are the important things to remember about the Volatility Tolerance Analysis:

- The three principles of sound investing are time horizon, diversification, and risk tolerance. The Volatility Tolerance Analysis addresses all three.
- The Volatility Tolerance Analysis measures your tolerance for risk and market volatility in each bucket, so we can create a Bucket Plan that stays within your comfort zone while simultaneously helping you reach your goals for long-term growth.
- This tool is different from the one most other advisors use because it measures your tolerance for volatility on Soon bucket money (money you may need sooner rather than later) and your Later bucket money (money with a longer investment time horizon).

Chapter 7

THE BUCKET PLAN® DESIGN

Bringing All the Elements Together for a Well-Planned Retirement

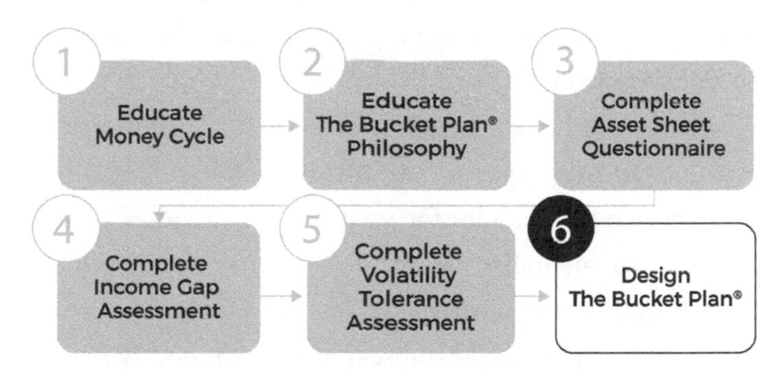

Now that we had a complete Asset Sheet Questionnaire, a complete Income Gap Assessment, and the results from the Volatility Tolerance Analysis, we could start designing Jerry and Irene's customized Bucket Plan with the confidence that we were moving in the right direction. They were eager to get the design process under way.

"Jerry and Irene, it ought to be clear by now how important

it is to segment or compartmentalize your assets for retirement into three different buckets based on your investment time horizon and your tolerance for volatility," I said. "To review, the first bucket—the Now bucket—contains money that is not invested and is typically made up of your emergency fund, sufficient money to cover planned expenses in the near future, and up to one year of income if you're about to retire. This is literally your money in the bank."

Irene said, "Yes, with the Now bucket money, we are willing to sacrifice an investment return in exchange for the comfort of knowing it's there when we need it."

"That's right," I said. "You've been paying attention."

"Yes I have," she said. "I'm actually digging this."

I couldn't help but notice Jerry's wide smile. He was clearly delighted by how much Irene was enjoying her newfound financial knowledge.

"The second bucket is the Soon bucket," I continued. "To determine the most appropriate investment strategies, portfolios, or investment vehicles for your unique situation, it is critical to compartmentalize the money you may need for income or withdrawals sooner rather than later and invest it more conservatively than you would the rest of your money. And why is that? Anybody?"

Irene replied, "Because doing so will buy us the time to confidently invest our remaining money in the third bucket, the Later bucket, for long-term growth, which can help us avoid running out of cash before we run out of years."

"You've got it!" I said.

"In summary, the Now bucket is typically the money you keep in the bank," I continued. "The Soon bucket is the money

Asset Sheet Questionnaire

Client 1 Name: Irene

Client 2 Name: Jerry Date: 10-14-14

BANK ACCOUNTS / CREDIT UNIONS (POST-TAX)

COMPANY NAME	OWNER	TYPE/ DUE DATE	POD / TOD DESIGNATION (Y/N)	PRIMARY / CONTINGENT BENEFICIARY	PER STIRPES / PER CAPITA	VALUE
ABC Credit Union	Joint	Checking	N	None	None	$2,000
Bank 5	Joint	Savings	N	None	None	$13,000
					SUB-TOTAL	$ 15,000

POST-TAX INVESTMENTS

ACCOUNT TYPE* /DUE DATE	COMPANY NAME	OWNER	POD / TOD DESIGNATION (Y/N)	PER STIRPES / PER CAPITA	COST BASIS	VALUE
* Brokerage Accounts, Annuities, Individual Stocks, Bonds, Mutual Funds, Alternative Investments, etc.						
Brokerage	UBS	Irene/Jerry	N	Per stirpes	$300,000	$350,000
					SUB-TOTAL	$ 350,000
					POST-TAX TOTAL	$ 365,000

that you may need sooner rather than later for income and withdrawals. The Later bucket is the money that you are confident you will not need for at least ten years or more. Now, let's design your Bucket Plan so you can see for yourself how simple—and how incredibly powerful—the process really is."

Bringing All the Elements Together

First, we referred to Jerry and Irene's Asset Sheet and started tallying up a few numbers so we would know the amount of liquid investable assets we had to work with. We started by writing down the $15,000 post-tax money they had in their bank account and the $350,000 post-tax investment in their joint brokerage account, and then we added those two numbers together. This told us that Jerry and Irene had a total of $365,000 in post-tax money.

POST-TAX ASSET SHEET PAGE

We carried out the same exercise with the pre-tax investments we'd cataloged on Jerry and Irene's Asset Sheet. Here, Jerry had $225,000 and Irene had $300,000 for a grand total of $525,000 in pre-tax money. It was important that we noted who owned each source of pre-tax money for two reasons, which I explained to Jerry and Irene.

"First, we cannot combine or mix your pre-tax money the way we can with post-tax. It has to be held separately in each of your respective accounts," I said. "Second, both of you will have required minimum distributions (RMDs) once you hit age seventy and a half. For planning purposes, we need to stay cognizant of how much pre-tax money each of you has because, if you miss an RMD, you'll be hit with a 50 percent tax penalty. You heard that correctly: 50 percent. For example, if your RMD is $20,000 and you fail to take it out on time, the IRS-calculated penalty will be $10,000! That's the last thing you want to have happen."

"You've got that right," Jerry said.

"I'm so glad we're going through this process," Irene said. "We may never have known about that kind of thing otherwise."

PRE-TAX INVESTMENTS							
*TAX STATUS	**ACCOUNT TYPE /DUE DATE	COMPANY NAME	OWNER	PRIMARY / CONTINGENT BENEFICIARY	PER STIRPES / PER CAPITA	COST BASIS	VALUE
* IRA, 401(k), 403(b), TSP, Pension, Other ** Brokerage Accounts, Annuities, Individual Stocks, Bonds, Mutual Funds, Alternative Investments, etc.							
Pre	403(b)	Community School District	Irene	N	per stirpes	$0	$250,000
Pre	IRA	UBS	Irene	N	per stirpes	$0	$50,000
Pre	401(k)	TIAA-CREF	Jerry	N	per stirpes	$0	$150,000
Pre	IRA	UBS	Jerry	N	per stirpes	$0	$75,000
			CLIENT 1 Irene		TOTAL	$	300,000
			CLIENT 2 Jerry		TOTAL	$	225,000
			TOTAL PRE-TAX INVESTMENTS			$	525,000

Next, we moved on to the Tax Favored Assets section of the Asset Sheet, where we'd recorded that Irene had accumulated $50,000 in a Roth IRA.

TAX FAVORED ASSETS								
*TAX STATUS	**ACCOUNT TYPE /DUE DATE	COMPANY NAME	OWNER	PRIMARY / CONTINGENT BENEFICIARY	PER STIRPES / PER CAPITA	COST BASIS	PENSION OR DEATH BENEFIT	VALUE
* Roth IRA, Roth 401(k), Roth 403(b), HSA, 529 Plan ** Brokerage Accounts, Annuities, Individual Stocks, Bonds, Mutual Funds, Alternative Investments, etc.								
Post	Roth	UBS	Irene	Jerry	Per stripes	n/a		$50,000
			CLIENT 1 Irene		TOTAL	$		$50,000
			CLIENT 2		TOTAL	$		
			TOTAL TAX FAVORED ASSETS			$		$50,000

The next page of the Asset Sheet refers to life insurance, which is relevant to The Bucket Plan® design only if there's cash value in the policy. In Jerry and Irene's case, there was $25,000 cash value in Irene's policy, plus death benefits of $100,000 on her and $300,000 on Jerry.

LIFE INSURANCE						
COMPANY NAME	PREMIUM	INSURED/ OWNER/ POLICY TYPE	PRIMARY / CONTINGENT BENEFICIARY	PER STIRPES / PER CAPITA	DEATH BENEFIT	CASH VALUE
Met Life	72 mo	Jerry	Irene (p)	Per Capita	300,000	
NYL	1200yr	Irene	Jerry (p)	Per Capita	100,000	25,000
				TOTAL DEATH BENEFIT	$	400,000
				TOTAL CASH VALUE	$	25,000

"The death benefits are important for your overall financial planning, and that's why we've increased Jerry's death benefit to pay off the second mortgage and possibly cover some of the tax liability from that pre-tax money you have," I said. "But death benefits are not important for designing your Bucket Plan for income creation, nor do we need to include any of the real estate, debt, or tax liability information from your Asset Sheet. All that data will be crucial for your overall planning, just not for this particular exercise."

At this point, we tallied all of Jerry and Irene's liquid investable assets: $365,000 post-tax; $525,000 pre-tax, $50,000 Roth, and $25,000 cash value life insurance for a grand total of $965,000.

Post-Tax		
Banks/Credit Unions	$	15,000
Investments	$	350,000
Total	$	365,000
Pre-Tax		
Client 1 - Irene	$	300,000
Client 2 - Jerry	$	225,000
Total	$	525,000
Tax Favored		
Client 1 - Irene	$	50,000
Client 2 -	$	
Total	$	50,000
Cash Value		
Client 1 - Irene	$	25,000
Client 2 -	$	
Total	$	25,000
Grand Total: Investable Assets	$	965,000
Income Gap Total:	$	(25,000)

"Now let's start allocating those assets by portioning them into the three buckets in your Bucket Plan," I said.

"The first thing we need to know is how much money you want to have set aside for emergencies and unplanned expenses in your checking and savings, so you can sleep soundly at night," I said. "This is your safe and liquid cash. As Irene pointed out earlier, with this money, you're willing to sacrifice the rate of return you would have earned if you had invested it. You know you won't even keep up with inflation with this money, but you don't care. It just makes you feel good that it's in the bank and easily accessible if you need it. So, what's your magic number?"

Jerry and Irene said they'd talked it over and decided that a $35,000 emergency fund would give them the most peace of mind. This was important because, per their Asset Sheet, they only had $15,000 in the bank at the time. We wrote $35,000 into the Now bucket for an emergency fund and talked about repositioning that amount from their $350,000 joint brokerage account.

The next part of the Now bucket is for planned expenses. Did Jerry and Irene have any substantial expenditures coming up in the next few years, such as a wedding, a kitchen remodel, or a roof on the house? I recalled Irene saying they planned to trade in their car soon, and they wanted to pay for the new one outright rather than financing it. We wrote that amount in the Now bucket under the "planned expense" category. They already had $15,000 in the bank, and with the value of their trade-in we didn't have to shuffle around any money to meet that expense.

"Jerry and Irene, now when it's time to buy your car, you won't have to worry about where the money will come from," I said. "You can rest assured that the expense is budgeted for and the money is there."

The next component of the Now bucket is income for the next twelve months. This didn't apply to Jerry and Irene because they were still working; they were not retiring for at least a year, probably two. But, had they been retiring then, we'd have put up to twelve months' worth of income in the Now bucket to bridge the gap until they were ready to start drawing from their Soon bucket.

"Remember," I said, "the customized Bucket Plan is adjusted to every individual's or couple's unique situation. No two plans are exactly alike."

We now turned our attention to filling the all-important Soon bucket, which would contain the couple's income for the first decade or so of retirement as well as an inflation hedge. They wanted to have no doubt whatsoever that this money would be there when they needed it; therefore, they didn't want to subject this allocation to any market volatility. What we needed to do here was set aside a certain amount of very conservative money to be earmarked for income purposes.

To determine that amount, we consulted Jerry and Irene's Income Gap Assessment, which showed that they would need to draw about $25,000 a year in income from their liquid investable assets during the first ten years of retirement. To come up with their ten-year aggregate, we simply multiplied $25,000 times ten years for a grand total of $250,000.

"Irene, I recommend earmarking the money from your 403(b) because you have the largest amount of pre-tax money," I explained. "Drawing from your pre-tax money will help limit your tax liability for the future. Because we drew from your pre-tax monies early when you were married-filing-jointly and had the benefit of better tax brackets, when one of you passes away, the survivor will be left with more post-tax money."

"And post-tax money is the 'good' money," Jerry said. "We want to hold on to that dough as long as we can."

"That's exactly right," I said. "We must also set aside some funds in the Soon bucket as a hedge against inflation that might lead to increases in the cost of your day-to-day essentials like bread, milk, gas, electricity—"

"And Girl Scout cookies," Jerry chimed in. "Because a life without Thin Mints and Do-Si-Dos is not a life worth living."

"No worries, Jerry," I laughed. "The rising price of Girl Scout cookies will be factored into your Bucket Plan."

For Jerry and Irene, we decided to reserve $75,000 as an inflation hedge, and we used Jerry's IRA to fund this portion of the bucket. Remember, we needed to draw from *both* Jerry's and Irene's IRAs because of the RMDs they would face in future years. Eventually the government would force them to take money out of their IRAs whether they wanted to or not; in this case, we would already be taking it out. By strategically repositioning a large portion of both of their IRAs into the Soon bucket and drawing from them early in retirement, we ensured that Jerry and Irene would meet those minimum distribution requirements with no problem. They wouldn't even have to think about it.

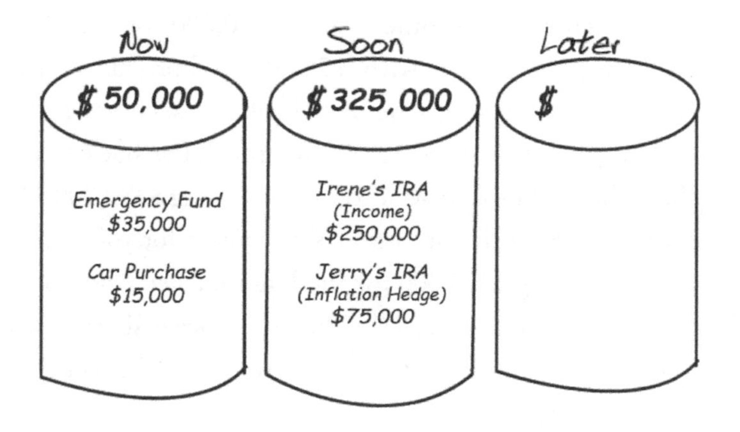

"Let's summarize what we have so far," I said. "You have $965,000 in liquid investable assets. We allocated $50,000 for your Now bucket and $325,000 for the Soon bucket.

Specifically, we will roll over $250,000 of Irene's 403(b) into an IRA for income out of the Soon bucket."

"Aren't there going to be tax consequences from doing that?" Irene asked.

"Nope," I replied. "There are no tax consequences. We will then roll over $75,000 of Jerry's IRA into an account earmarked as an inflation hedge in the Soon bucket to provide additional income to you as the years go by. The remaining $590,000 will be put into the Later bucket. This is the money we will position with an eye for long-term growth. We will also look at legacy-planning options to try to reduce your tax liability and protect your assets for the future. We'll fill this bucket as follows.

"Irene, recall that you started with $300,000 of pre-tax money," I continued, "and $250,000 of that went into the Soon bucket for retirement income, leaving $50,000 for the Later bucket. Jerry, you started with $225,000 of pre-tax money, $75,000 of which went into the Soon bucket to serve as a hedge against inflation, leaving $150,000 for the Later bucket. You also have the joint brokerage account containing $350,000. We will put $35,000 of that into the Now bucket for your emergency fund, leaving $315,000 for the Later bucket. And finally, Irene's $50,000 Roth and $25,000 life insurance cash value will go into the Later bucket. Here's how your final Bucket Plan will look on paper."

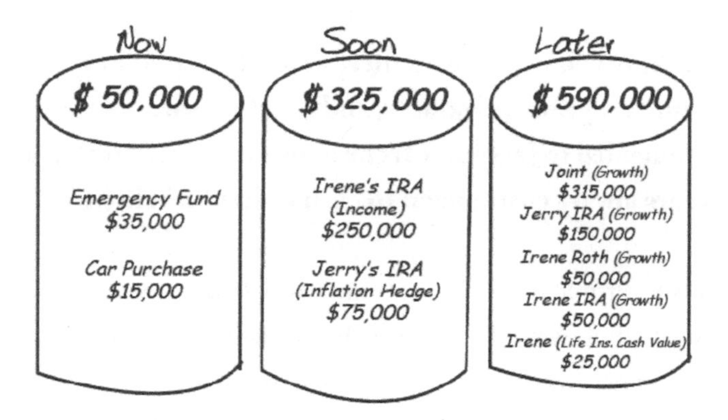

"Jerry and Irene, all of your liquid investable assets are now strategically positioned to meet your needs in the now, soon, and later time frames," I said. "By setting up a Soon bucket with which we will be very conservative, you've mitigated the threat of running out of money by eliminating sequence of returns risk from your plan. You can be confident you've done your best to defuse tax time bombs for each other and the kids because you'll be drawing heavily from your already taxed pre-tax money, while letting the Roth IRA—post-tax money—and the cash value in your life insurance grow for the future. That's a big deal, to be drawing $25,000 a year from your pre-tax money with only a $40 a month income tax liability. At our next meeting, we'll dive into the specific products and portfolios that make the most sense for you in each bucket."

"I'm looking forward to that," Jerry said. "We can't thank you enough, Jason. I'm going to sleep like a baby tonight. It's such a relief to know that we've finally got a sound plan for the future. And I love having all our financial information gathered in one place so we can get to it quickly whenever we need it. I'll see you next week!"

I won't bore you with the nuances of all the different investment options, products, and portfolios we recommended to Jerry and Irene at our next meeting because those are always customized to each individual client.

As the three of us shook hands and said our goodbyes that day, we had no way of knowing that Irene would need to access that information so soon. But as heartbreaking as the outcome was for these folks, I'm comforted by the knowledge that they left our office with the confidence that, should life deal them a difficult hand—as it unfortunately would with Jerry's untimely death less than a year later—the surviving spouse, Irene, would have peace of mind and financial security for the rest of her life.

RECAP

There are three purposes for the "safe and liquid" money in the Now bucket:

- Your emergency fund (however much makes you feel comfortable, your magic number).
- Short-term planned expenses (a roof for the house, a wedding, college tuition for a child or a grandchild, a new car, and so on).
- Income for up to the next twelve months, if you are retired or close to retiring.

The more "conservative" money in the Soon bucket has three purposes:

- Conservative growth not subject to sequence of returns risk due to market risk and interest rate risk.
- Income or withdrawals for the first phase of retirement, or to plan for forced income due to required minimum distributions (RMDs).
- An inflation hedge to provide increases in your income as things become more expensive in the future.

And the "long-term growth and legacy-planning" money in the Later bucket has three purposes:

- Growth and income for the second phase of retirement through the rest of your life.

- Building a tax efficient legacy for yourself, your surviving spouse or other beneficiaries, or a charity.
- Long-term care/disability funds (chronic care) to pay for health-care expenses throughout the rest of your life.

Chapter 8

HOW DOES YOUR CURRENT PLAN STACK UP?

A Few Important Questions and a Scorecard Assessment

Now that you know the power of The Bucket Plan® planning process, do you share Jerry and Irene's confidence that your existing financial plan will be able to meet your needs far into the future? Ask yourself these questions:

- Do my current allocations plan for and mitigate market risk, interest rate risk, and sequence of returns risk?
- Do my current asset allocations consider the money cycle and the preservation phase?
- Do I have a Soon bucket in place to meet my needs in the early stage of retirement?
- Does my current plan proactively defuse tax time bombs?

If you're like most retirees, your answers to these questions will be a resounding "no . . . not by a long shot."

Now take a minute to assess your current financial health by filling out our Bucket Plan Scorecard. This Scorecard is a valuable tool that will help you pinpoint any specific areas of your financial life that need improvement as of today. To download a digital copy, visit TheBucketPlanBook.com.

The Bucket Plan® Scorecard

Name: ____________ **Date:** ____________

Truths	1 2 3	4 5 6	7 8 9	10 11 12	Score
Well-coordinated Team of Professionals	I don't have a team, but I'm sure I can figure this all out on my own when I need to.	I get some tax help and investment advice, but there may be some gaps in my plan.	I have an accountant, advisor, attorney, and insurance agent, but they don't coordinate with each other.	I have a full financial, tax planning, and legal team, and they all work well together.	
Proactive Income Tax Planning	April 15 is panic time, and taxes are usually a big surprise.	I generally understand how to save on taxes, but there are many things I do not know.	I use a tax preparer, but they don't provide proactive tax planning advice or strategies.	I work with tax-planning professionals who test multiple scenarios and show me how to save money on taxes.	
Healthcare Expense Funding Planned	I don't know what my insurance or healthcare costs will be, and there are major gaps in my plan.	I have health insurance and Medicare covered, but I am not sure if I've saved enough.	I have enough savings to cover basics, but no plan for long-term care, assisted living, or home healthcare.	My plan accounts for all medical costs, and I have sufficient income and assets to cover my healthcare needs.	
Legacy Planning & Documented Organization	If I died tomorrow, my family would have no idea about taxes, legal fees, or how to settle the estate.	I think my assets are titled correctly and beneficiaries are current, but I have no other plans in place for when I pass.	I'm fairly organized, but my family would be stressed to figure out how to settle affairs.	Everything is organized and documented, and there's a clear map to settle affairs with minimal taxes and legal costs.	
				Subtotal	

Truths	1	2	3	4	5	6	7	8	9	10	11	12	Score
A Documented Financial Plan that's Fully Understood	I have no plan and don't really know how to get started.			I definitely know a plan is important, but I don't have one in place yet.			I have a plan...I don't fully understand it, but I hope my advisor does.			I have a plan. It's completely documented, and I fully understand how it works.			
Assets are Segmented Based on Time & Purpose	I've been sold various financial products, but I don't understand them all and could lose a lot in any market correction.			I don't really know how much risk I'm taking with my investments or which accounts to draw income from in retirement.			I've got stocks, bonds, or mutual funds, but don't know how market risk, interest rates or sequence of returns will affect me.			My assets are fully segmented in different buckets and invested according to time horizon and the purpose of the money.			
Stable & Sustainable Lifetime Income	Social Security is my only stable income, and my assets will not generate enough income to meet my needs.			I am or will be spending more than 5% of investment assets to meet my income needs in retirement.			My basic living expenses are covered by stable and sustainable lifetime income sources.			All my income needs are covered by stable and sustainable lifetime income sources. I'm set!			
Peace of Mind	I'm worried that I won't have enough money to last in retirement or survive a market downturn.			I've probably saved enough to last in retirement, but I'm not sure about my spouse or family after I'm gone.			I've saved enough money to provide for my and my family's lifetime, but there are some loose ends I'd like to tie up.			I have confidence and clarity that all aspects of my financial and estate situation are under complete control.			
												Subtotal (back)	
												Subtotal (front)	
												Total Score	

What's your result? A score of less than 80 means you have some serious gaps that must be addressed. If that's your situation, then you need to engage with a Bucket Plan advisor to create your own customized plan, and you need to do it soon.

Need Additional Help?

Jason Smith and his training organization, Clarity 2 Prosperity, provide regular live training opportunities to qualified financial advisors to earn The Bucket Plan® Certification. Advisors who achieve this certification have completed an online course and test, and one and a half days of hands-on training and passed a proctored exam verifying they have mastered each of the steps and tools described in this book, including how to:

- Teach the money cycle, sequence of returns risk, and The Bucket Plan philosophy
- Uncover, subcategorize, and inventory all assets through the Asset Sheet Questionnaire
- Identify supplemental income needs through the Income Gap Assessment
- Determine risk comfort level for each bucket through the Volatility Tolerance Analysis
- Design an income plan coordinating insurance and investments
- Represent a best interest standard for you as the client through this planning process

To find an advisor in your area who has The Bucket Plan Certification along with additional resources for The Bucket Plan, visit TheBucketPlanBook.com today!

SUMMARY

So, there you have it—a simple, three-bucket approach to structuring your assets to provide reliable income when you need it and to grow your money to outpace inflation throughout retirement. Your customized Bucket Plan will make it possible for you to enjoy your retirement while worrying less about the volatility of the stock market and interest rates, or the potentially devastating hazard of sequence of returns risk.

By segmenting your money into three different buckets based on your investment time horizon, volatility tolerance, and income need, you can eliminate certain risks and avoid making bad decisions that could cause you to run out of money. You'll defuse tax time bombs and make it possible for your surviving spouse to live the rest of his or her life in comfort. You'll make it possible for your loved ones to settle your affairs with relative ease when the time comes, and you'll also be able to rest assured that you haven't unintentionally disinherited your grandkids. Utilizing a Soon bucket to preserve some of the money you've worked so hard to accumulate will allow you to draw income if/when you need it (or are forced to take it via RMDs) while simultaneously buying a time horizon to invest the rest for growth. You'll be a calm, rational, confident investor who lets the markets work for you rather than trying to compete against them.

But, best of all, you'll be able to sleep soundly at night because you'll know you have a financial plan that covers all the bases. When you work with a holistic financial planner to strategically position your assets in a Bucket Plan, you get peace of mind . . . and there's no greater asset on earth than that.

SUMMARY

INDEX

D

E

F

G

H

I

M

N

O

P

R

S

T

U

V

W

ABOUT THE AUTHOR

Jason L Smith is a nationally-acclaimed speaker, financial planner, author, coach, and entrepreneur. Following in his father's footsteps as a second-generation advisor, he founded his financial services practice, The JL Smith Group, in 1995 to provide clients with holistic financial planning services that align investments, insurance, taxes, and estate planning into one comprehensive, coordinated plan. After a serious heart diagnosis at the age of twenty-nine, Jason made a commitment to transition his personal financial planning firm into a process-driven company so it could continue with or without him. Today, his financial planning practice is self-managing, allowing him to provide focused financial planning services to his clients.

With the overriding goal of improving the lives of American families through holistic financial planning, Jason utilizes his experiences as an accomplished advisor to train and mentor other advisors through live training events, monthly coaching calls and study groups. To better fulfill this mission, he founded Clarity 2 Prosperity, a financial training, coaching and IP development organization for financial advisors, where he currently serves as president and CEO. He also founded and serves as the chairman for Prosperity Capital Advisors, an SEC-registered investment advisory firm and C2P Advisory Group, an insurance marketing organization. Together, the three firms work to help advisors and institutions nationwide to simplify holistic financial planning in order to provide financial solutions in the best interest of their clients.

Jason regularly speaks at exclusive industry events including Ed Slott's Elite IRA Advisor Group℠ workshops, Forum 400, and MDRT's Top of the Table annual meeting. He was recognized as an Emerging Leader and Legend at Forum 400, a member only insurance industry organization; he was named as one of *Investment News* Top 40 Under 40 Industry Standouts and honored with his picture on the cover of the publication; and he received an honorable mention for Best Rising Star by *National Underwriter Life & Health* magazine. He consistently serves as a national media resource and has authored several advisor-facing books, including *Clarity 2 Prosperity: An Advisor's Guide to Charging Fees for Holistic Planning* and is co-author of *The Hiring Advantage*. Jason has been featured on public television for his leadership in moving the industry toward providing fully holistic services for the benefit of all clients.

Jason is an Investment Advisor Representative and a Certified Estate Planner™ (CEP®) through the National Institute of Certified Estate Planners, and he holds his Certification for Long-Term Care Planning (CLTC) from the CLTC Board of Standards. He is a member of Ed Slott's Master Elite IRA Advisor Group℠, an exclusive IRA study group of financial professionals who are committed to the study and mastery of IRA planning. As a member, Jason has participated in numerous training workshops on individual retirement accounts and has been mentored by nationally-acclaimed IRA expert, Ed Slott, CPA.

Jason enjoys spending time with his wife Holly; daughter Jordan; and twins Wyatt and Berkley. Committed to helping others, he volunteers for philanthropic endeavors and with a number of charitable organizations. This has included taking international service projects abroad to help impoverished communities and leading a national campaign with Soles-4Souls, collecting 25,000 pairs of shoes to distribute to those in need. In his spare time, he enjoys cooking, yoga, fitness and outdoor activities such as hiking, kayaking, mountain climbing, and snowmobiling.